ROME

By the staff of Berlitz Guides

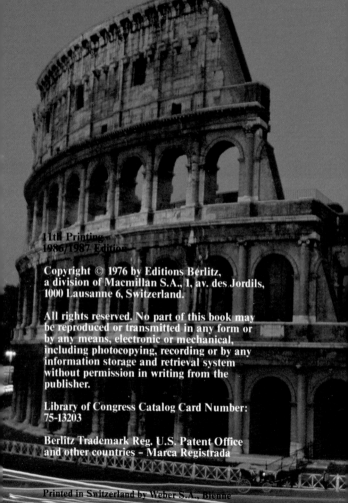

How to use our guide

- All the practical information, hints and tips that you will need before and during the trip start on page 95, with a complete rundown of contents on page 99.

- For general background, see the sections Rome and the Romans, p. 6, and A Brief History, p. 10.

- All the sights to see are listed between pages 18 and 69, with suggestions on excursions and day trips from Rome from page 70–77. Our own choice of sights most highly recommended is pinpointed by the Berlitz traveller symbol.

- Entertainment, nightlife and other leisure activities are described between pages 78 to 82 and 92 to 94, while information on restaurants and cuisine is to be found on pages 83 to 91.

- Finally, there is an index at the back of the book, pp. 126–128.

Text: Don Larrimore
Photography: Herbert Fried
We would like to thank Dr. Giannino Rigolio, Aideen Archbold, the Italian National Tourist office, and Mr. Enzo Luongo, for their valuable assistance.
Cartography: Falk-Verlag, Hamburg.

Contents

Cover picture: St. Peter's Square

Rome
and the Romans

Above all, it's the contrasts of Rome that overwhelm a visitor. It is at once an incredible mingling of ancient and modern, religious and profane, serene and chaotic. Sprawling today ever farther beyond its original seven hills and the banks of the serpentine River Tiber, Rome amazes, delights and at times exasperates.

No city in the world is a more complete museum of human endeavour. Stark ruins bear imposing witness to Rome's great empire of centuries long past. In her myriad palaces and churches are found enough artistic treasures to consume a lifetime of sightseeing. Within the ancient city walls, any cobblestoned street reveals a fountain, a marble bust, a fresco, a piazza, a hidden courtyard—each telling a tiny fragment of the intriguing story of the Eternal City.

Mostly, today's Romans are indifferent to their magnificent surroundings. Yet they themselves help make the city so fascinating; their emotional behaviour and physiognomy recall their forbears at least as far back as the Renaissance.

Gesticulating constantly, hurling harmlessly barbed insults, religiously staying out of the sun, irreligiously whispering at mass, honking their horns over a football victory, parading in demonstrations, triple-parking their Fiats, gulping down espressos, pampering their babies, the Romans demonstrably live and love life to the fullest.

Always vibrant and on the go, Rome is very much an outdoor city where emotions are on public display. The texture of life seems as torrid as the Roman sun, but it isn't really. The everyday theatrical blustering over a scraped car or a street vendor's overpriced watermelon sounds vastly more menacing than it is. A pretty girl may be whistled at, flattered, followed or perhaps (infrequently these days) even pinched, but the exuberance of Rome's young Lotharios is rarely sinister.

Rome is a white-helmeted policeman turning his back on a clamorous traffic jam to

Against monumental backdrops, monumental traffic jams.

crowds swarm through the flea market at Porta Portese and jam St. Peter's Square at noon for the pope's benediction.

As the seat of the papacy, Rome is a compelling spiritual magnet for some 550 million Roman Catholics. The in-

Left: *Romans of all ages turn out for May Day parade.* Below: *A favourite pastime in Rome—amore.*

watch a beautiful woman glide down the street.

For six days a week, the Eternal City is infernally noisy and crowded. And nowadays, with the traditional post-lunch siesta distinctly on the wane, the streets are ebullient and full all day long. On Sundays, however, as churchbells peal, the centre of Rome is shuttered and deserted, though colourful

fluence of the Holy See on the municipality of Rome, which totally surrounds it, is inescapable.

The first of the pope's nine titles is Bishop of Rome (*Vescovo di Roma*), and his Easter message *Urbi et Orbi* is addressed first to the city and then to the world. Priests, nuns, bishops and cardinals are seen throughout the city, which boasts some 500 churches; many of Rome's most majestic palaces are the property of the Vatican; church orphanages, clinics, schools, mission houses, cloisters and seminaries abound.

And yet, after long centuries as a papal capital, Rome today is primarily the secular capital of a struggling nation, caught up in a maelstrom of politics and commerce. Blue-black government sedans carry ministers and senators through the traffic jams. In tapestried dining-rooms rotund executives discuss oil deals and film contracts over spaghetti and Chianti. The President of the Republic lays a wreath or receives a monarch. In spite of political troubles, which have tended recently to take a tragic turn, life carries on virtually unchanged.

The bustle of today is, of course, only the merest echo of Rome's tempestuous yesterdays when she was the centre of western civilization. But the city's art, its books, its museums and venerable stones themselves bespeak an incomparable legacy to mankind, reminding the visitor that Rome is truly the City of the World.

The Eternal City

Rome lies between the hills on the one side, and the sea, about 20 kilometres away, on the other. Built originally on the famous seven hills, it spread outwards in both directions to cover its present 410 square miles with a population of around 3.5 million.

Seventeen hundred years ago, Rome's population was about one million, its area perhaps a fifth of the present-day size. Encircled by two defensive walls (partly intact today), imperial Rome had 11 aqueducts, 10 basilicas, two amphitheatres, 11 forums, two circuses, 190 granaries, only two general markets, 11 baths, 36 arches and 1,150 fountains.

Then, as now, the initialled seal of Rome was visible throughout the city —S.P.Q.R., which stands for *Senatus Populusque Romanus,* the Senate and People of Rome, denoting the theoretical equality of both in decisions of state.

A Brief History

The symbol of Rome.

Nowhere are the triumphs and tragedies of western civilization more vividly mirrored than in the history of Rome—all 2,700 years of it. Cherished legend has it that Rome was founded divinely in 753 B.C. by Romulus who, with his twin brother Remus, was said to have been born of the god Mars and a vestal virgin. Abandoned on the Palatine Hill, Romulus and Remus were suckled by a she-wolf. To this day, the mother wolf remains Rome's city symbol. April 21 is celebrated as the anniversary of the capital's founding by Romulus who finally, the tradition goes, ascended to heaven.

In fact, settlements of Latin and Sabine tribes, clustered in the hilly area around the River Tiber in the eighth century B.C., were gradually dominated by the mysterious Etruscans. They established there a dynasty of kings which ruled for two and a half centuries.

Roman Expansion

In 510 B.C., the Romans successfully revolted, abolishing the Etruscan royalty and establishing a republic which endured for 500 years.

Strengthened by the steady settling of internal conflicts and by overriding loyalty to their city-state, Romans displayed great tenacity in defending and extending their power by force of arms. After the whole Italian peninsula had been brought under their sway, they struggled for over 100 years in the Punic wars (264 to 146 B.C.) to defeat the great commercial and naval power of Carthage. The resulting victory for Rome gave her control over the commerce of the Mediterranean, over Sicily, Sardinia, Spain and the northern shores of Africa.

From this one city, the conquering soldiers—carrying with

them Roman administration and language, developing cities, leaving indelible traces of their civilization—reached out into what is now Spain and France, across the Rhine and into Britain. Why, for example, is London the administrative capital of Britain today? Because the Romans chose to make it so. Where did the plan come from to build Hadrian's Wall across the grey, wind-swept neck of land that separates England from Scotland? From this southern, sun-drenched city of Rome.

The six major military Roman roads, fanning out like the spokes of a wheel from the capital—Appia, Latina, Salaria, Flaminia, Aurelia and Cassia—were built with cobbled paving stones and parallel foot-paths between 361 and 108 B.C. Somewhat less bumpy today, thanks to more recent resurfacing, they're still in use with the same names. However, modern traffic moves not much faster than a Roman chariot.

The Republic, an aristocratic commonwealth under consuls and the all-powerful senate, thrived on the civic obedience of its plebeians and the imaginative leadership of its

Julius Caesar—the noblest Roman.

educated patricians. But in the century before the birth of Jesus Christ, violent civil wars fatally weakened the republican régime.

In 49 B.C., after crossing a central-Italian stream called the Rubicon, Julius Caesar, general, orator and politician, became in effect the monarch of Rome. He planned a radical reorganization of the governmental structure, but after only five years in power, years of endless intrigue, Caesar was assassinated by Brutus and other toga-clad nobles.

In the ensuing anarchy, the Republic finally collapsed and, in 27 B.C. the Roman Empire was born under Caesar's legal heir, Octavian, who became Emperor Augustus Caesar. 11

Augustus restored order, and for the 40 years of his reign Rome knew the peak of its glory. The capital's monumental buildings glittered in marble, peace prevailed throughout the far-flung Empire, and the golden age of Latin letters brought forth such giants as Horace, Ovid, Livy and Virgil.

Tens of thousands of foreigners, many slaves or poor labourers, flooded into Rome. This was around the time of Christ, and among the various new religions carried to Rome by these penniless immigrants was Christianity. In July of A.D. 64, during the rule of the notoriously dissolute Emperor Nero, most of Rome burned down. The blame was placed on the Christians, imperially viewed as the most persistently troublesome sect within the large Jewish community in the city. Vast numbers of Christians were rounded up and killed, martyrs whose catacomb tombs are reverently preserved to this day.

Most prominent among the victims were Christ's apostles, St. Paul and possibly St. Peter. According to tradition, Peter ministered to followers of the new faith in the capital of an essentially hostile empire.

With Peter began the succession of bishops, presbyters and, later, popes which has continued uninterruptedly until the present.

Decline

Despite the efforts of a handful of concerned emperors, by the fourth century the Empire was in full decline, succumbing to military drains on resources, famine and plague. As many as 150,000 Romans at a time lived on a dole of free corn.

Corruption and indolence debased the emperors' rule, and invasions by barbarian Germanic hordes hastened the end. In 283 the Forum was almost totally destroyed by fire, never to recover its full magnificence.

As the result of a spiritual vision, the Emperor Constantine embraced Christianity as the official religion of the Empire. In 331 he removed the imperial seat to Byzantium (Constantinople). Proud to build a new capital for himself, and possibly expecting it to be easier to establish Christianity there rather than in traditionally pagan Rome, Constantine chose a site which was crucial for the defence of the Empire against attack from the East. His move effectively split the Empire between east and west. The schism in the Christian church remains to this day.

The Dark Ages

As the Empire declined, the practice was adopted of recruiting its most formidable enemies to help defend it against other outsiders. But the dangers of such a course were to be demonstrated in violent fashion when the hired defenders themselves turned attackers. In 476, Odovacar, chief of the barbarian Heruli, forced the last Roman emperor, Romulus Augustulus, to abdicate, finishing off the classical western empire. Not until 1870 would Italy again be politically united. Odovacar was killed by the Ostrogoths, commanded by Theodoric, who ruled Italy from Ravenna, not Rome. Eventually the popes gained control over the "Duchy of Rome".

The succeeding three centuries, known as the Dark Ages for Rome and Europe, saw more incursions across the Alps by other Germanic tribes —Goths, Lombards and Franks. The once-mighty city became a ravaged provincial village. Its small surviving population clustered in the marshy districts along the Tiber, having deserted the seven hills after the invaders cut the imperial aqueducts.

Meanwhile, the prestige of the papacy steadily increased.

2,000-year-old paving stones, smoothed by centuries of use.

In an era of peril and confusion the church was a repository of tradition and learning. During the Dark Ages, it carried the sole torch of hope for the eventual dispersion of barbarism. Papal authority was enormously boosted by the appearance of the so-called "Donation of Constantine". Though later found to be a forgery, for centuries it was believed authentic. In it the emperor granted the popes political power over Rome and all Italy when he left for his New Rome, Byzantium.

On Christmas Day, 800, in St. Peter's Basilica, Pope Leo III crowned the Frankish king, Charlemagne, first emperor of the Holy Roman Empire. The joint though often bitterly acrimonious stewardship of the western world under pope and emperor was to last for ten centuries, but it was not an empire which rested on a single military and political power. It was a far cry from the might of the Caesars.

Over the next 400 years came invasions by Saracens and Magyars, Saxons and Normans, with papal Rome struggling along as only one of many feudal city-states on the tormented peninsula. Starting in 1095, popes began calling Europe's Christian princes to the long series of crusades aimed at removing the infidels from Jerusalem and the Holy Places. But by the 14th century Rome had degenerated into a state of chaos—deplored by Dante in his *Divine Comedy*—and the seat of the papacy was moved to Avignon in 1309, remaining under the protection of the French kings for 68 years.

The Renaissance

Finally re-established in Rome, the popes harshly put down all local resistance to their rule. Yet during the 15th and 16th centuries, the papacy also became a notable patron of the Renaissance, that remarkable effusion of great art and intellectual endeavour which gloriously transformed medieval Rome and indelibly affected western culture.

Pope Eugene IV (1431-47) summoned Florentine humanists and artists to work at the Vatican; popes Nicholas V (1447-55), Sixtus IV (1471-84), Julius II (1503-13) and Leo X (1513-21), a member of the renowned Florentine Medici family, promoted the vast outpouring of neo-classical art and collected treasures proudly displayed today in the Vatican Museum.

The architect Bramante designed the new St. Peter's Basilica, which took all of the 16th century to erect; Raphael painted masterpieces in the apostolic palaces; Michelangelo's frescoes made the Sistine Chapel the jewel of Renaissance art.

The exuberant life of Renaissance Rome was brutally snuffed out in May, 1527, by mutinous troops of the invading Hapsburg emperor (and Spanish king), Charles V. It was the last—and worst—sack of the city.

Foreign Domination

Spanish control over the peninsula was to last until the 18th century. Meanwhile the position of the papacy and the doctrines of the Church of Rome were being challenged by Luther, Calvin and other leaders of the Reformation.

In the face of these challenges and setbacks, enthusiastic popes saw to it that Rome was rebuilt even more magnificently: its 16th- and 17th-century palaces, churches and fountains remain the city's landmarks even today. And despite foreign domination, Rome again became the artistic centre of the world, the age producing such giants as the sculptor Gian Lorenzo Bernini (1598-1680) and the composers Monteverdi (1567-1643) and Palestrina (1525-94).

In the early 18th century, the authority over Italy which Spain had been exercising passed to Austria. For a time, this Austrian supremacy was interrupted by Napoleon, who invaded Italy in 1796 and who abolished the anachronistic Holy Roman Empire in 1806. During the French occupation there began to develop a national self-awareness in Italy, and when Austrian rule was re-established after Napoleon, it was challenged by some of the Italians themselves. Many people looked to Pope Pius IX to lead this nationalist movement, but he declined to come out against such a major Catholic power as Austria. In 1848, when a republic was set up in Rome by Mazzini in the cause of Italian nationalism, the pope fled the city. He returned only after the 15

republic had been crushed by the French army in 1849.

Unification of most of Italy was eventually achieved in the 1860s, through the shrewd diplomacy of Cavour, the heroics of Garibaldi, and the leadership of King Victor Emmanuel of Piedmont (a state centred on Turin). But Rome itself was not captured until 1870, when the French troops which had been guarding it were withdrawn. Rome then became the capital of the new Kingdom of Italy, a constitutional monarchy. Pope Pius IX, left in possession of only the Vatican, the mother church of St. John Lateran and a summer palace at Castel Gandolfo, declared himself to be "a prisoner of the monarchy". For half a century the

Giuseppe Garibaldi, the Italian patriot who unified his country.

popes remained shut away in the Vatican. They were not so much prisoners of the monarchy as of the fact that for hundreds of years their predecessors had chosen to rule not only the Catholic church but also a small state in the center of Italy.

The 20th Century

Despite the excitement at the time of the unification, democracy failed to become firmly established in Italy. Crisis followed crisis, and people lost confidence in the government. During World War I, Italy fought on the side of Britain and France against Germany and Austria, but afterwards she felt she had been insufficiently rewarded for her sacrifices. As parliamentary democracy disintegrated, Benito Mussolini's fascists seized power in 1922. Seven years later Mussolini *(il Duce)* concluded the Lateran Agreements with the papacy, which created the independent state of the Vatican City and recognized Catholicism as Italy's national religion.

Mussolini's régime littered Rome's venerable landscape with starkly modern architectural creations. But also, by linking Italy's fate to that of Hitler's Germany, it dragged the country into defeat in World War II. Mussolini himself was forced from power in 1943 and was later killed by Italian partisans. Rome fortunately escaped being the scene of major fighting and was captured by the Allies in June 1944 with its treasures intact.

In June 1946, Italy voted in a referendum to abolish the monarchy and establish the democratic republic which exists today. Joining in the grouping of states which became the European Economic Community, Italy also experienced a considerable postwar upsurge of productivity and wealth, although the huge problem of the poor southern part of the country, the Mezzogiorno, continues to this day. Political stability has also yet to be achieved. But through triumphs and setbacks alike, Rome, the Eternal City, continues to receive its visitors as one of the great centres of the history of mankind.

17

What to See

It's patently no exaggeration to say, as city fathers have for centuries, that Rome itself is a museum. Indoors and outdoors, and even underground, there's far too much to see in a year, let alone on a short holiday. Rome has 58 museums and public galleries and 32 sites officially classified as ancient monuments.

Clearly, the wise visitor will be carefully selective as he roams over Rome's 410 square miles. And no matter how long he stays, roam he certainly should, on foot whenever possible. While there

---

Instant Rome

For those making only a very brief visit, the very highest of Rome's highlights certainly include:

St. Peter's Basilica
Vatican Museum
Roman Forum
Colosseum
Piazza Navona
Old Rome
Borghese Gallery
Michelangelo's *Moses*
Trevi Fountain
Spanish Steps

---

are buses, taxis, chauffeured limousines, horse-drawn carriages and an underground (subway), nothing beats walking in this astonishing city.

Nonetheless, anyone making his first visit to Rome is best advised to begin with an orientation tour by bus. All large travel agencies conduct daily tours with informative commentaries on major sights by guides who speak a variety of languages. These reasonably priced tours normally last about three hours and can be booked by any hotel desk-clerk. There's no better way to get one's bearings before exploring Rome's wonders more closely.

Rome is in a constant state of upheaval. A tremendous restoration job is underway, monuments are whisked away, then replaced; scaffolding is put up and pulled down. Don't be too disappointed if what you're looking for is not there or not visible. It will be next visit.

Sightseeing without Tears

Many tourists find their energy drained by the often oppressive heat of the Roman summer. They needn't: plan to do outdoor sightseeing on foot in the cooler early morning and late afternoon hours, and choose *air-conditioned* buses for the orientation tours ("forced ventilation" may be lukewarm).

Air-conditioned cafés are fairly scarce, but Rome's churches, some of which will surely be on your itinerary, even accidentally, are remarkably cool havens on the hottest day, and as you linger, there'll always be something beautiful to look at. You'll notice Romans deliberately—and slowly—walking on the shady side of the street even if it takes them a bit out of their way. The good sense of that will quickly become evident: striding across a large piazza in the midday sun can leave you drenched and wilted.

If you're caught away from your own hotel and craving to cool down and freshen up, Rome has half a dozen conveniently located "daytime hotels" (see *Alberghi diurni* in the yellow pages of the telephone book). This helpful, legitimate institution offers shower and bathroom facilities, manicure, hairdressing, clothes pressing, left luggage (baggage check) and other services.

Lunch break for carrozza *horses—and their drivers.*

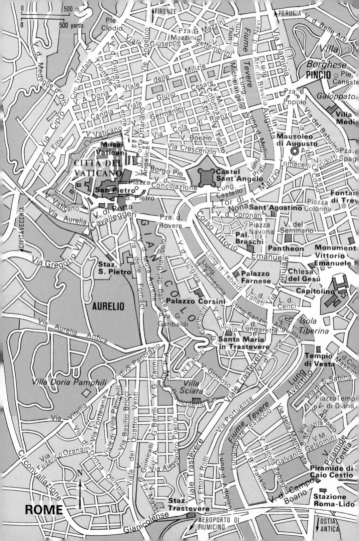

♟ Vatican City
(Città del Vaticano)

To see it can only be to marvel at it. The tiny* sovereign state of Vatican City contains not only the residence of the pope, the world's largest church and a most impressive square, but many of mankind's greatest treasures as well.

In centuries long past, the area that is now the seat of Roman Catholicism was at times a malarial swamp and even a simple cow pasture. Julius Caesar planned a sports arena here, Augustus Caesar built a huge basin for boat festivals, and under today's St. Peter's Square Nero erected a circus where countless early Christian martyrs were tortured and crucified.

Many scholars believe the martyrdom of St. Peter took place in Nero's infamous circus. During the fourth century, on the nearby site of the apostle's tomb, the Emperor Constantine erected the original St. Peter's Basilica which survived intact five centuries of barbarian invasions until 846 when it was sacked by marauding Saracens. Pope Leo IV then ordered massive walls built around the sacred church and the enclosed area became known as the Leonine City or Vatican City.

For the past six centuries (since 1377), the Vatican has been the official residence of the popes, but it wasn't until the Lateran Pact of February 11, 1929 (see HISTORY, page 17), that it became a sovereign state independent of Italy.

Symbolically guarded (since 1506) by an élite corps of friendly Swiss guards*, Vatican City has a population of about 300, including the pope and the cardinals. About 4,000 commute to work from across the "border", which is a broad band painted on the street at the rim of St. Peter's Square. The tiny Vatican railway station hasn't been used since 1962, when Pope John XXIII set out on a pilgrimage to Assisi and Loreto. As Stalin noted to Churchill, the Vatican has no army. Its diplomats accredited around the world rely on the spiritual and moral influence of the pope—an influence hardly negligible even in today's world of power politics.

---

* 108 acres.

* For centuries the Swiss were Europe's bravest and most loyal mercenary soldiers, usually in the service of France.

ST. PETER'S SQUARE
(Piazza San Pietro)

Opening out as if to embrace all mankind, this awesomely immense masterpiece was designed and completed in less than 12 years (1655-67) by Rome's leading baroque sculptor, Gian Lorenzo Bernini. The quadruple colonnade has 284 travertine columns, 88 pilasters and 140 statues. To appreciate Bernini's incomparable achievement in symmetry, be sure to stand on one of the two round, green paving stones flanking the square's central

Faithful throng St. Peter's Square to receive the papal benediction.

The Pope

Though he's a busy head of church and state, it is possible to see the pope in person.

When he's in residence at the Vatican, the pope normally holds a public audience every Wednesday at 11 a.m. (at 5 p.m. in summer). An invitation to this ceremony (in the Papal Audience Hall to the left of the basilica) may be obtained from the Pontifical Prefect's Office through the bronze gates of St. Peter's Square, which is open Tuesday and Wednesday mornings. Semi-private audiences with the pope are arranged through a visitor's bishop at home. On Sundays at noon, the pope appears at the window of the papal apartments in the Apostolic Palace (to the right of the basilica, overlooking St. Peter's Square), delivers a brief homily over a loudspeaker system, says the angelus and blesses the crowd below. On a few major holy days during the year, the pontiff celebrates high mass in St. Peter's.

obelisk—the four rows of columns will then, astonishingly, appear as a single row. Behind the colonnade is the Vatican post office; its dramatic stamps are a collector's delight.

The square's ancient Egyptian obelisk (84 feet high) was once the goal post of Nero's Circus. In 1586, it took 900 men with 140 horses and 44 winches over four months to raise the pillar into place.

At Easter or on other high religious occasions, as many as 300,000 people jam into St. Peter's Square, which is 247 yards across at its widest point. The effect of the vast elliptical space is to draw the eye towards Michelangelo's monumental dome atop St. Peter's.

ST. PETER'S BASILICA
(Basilica di San Pietro)

The largest Catholic church ever built was consecrated on November 18, 1626, a complete reconstruction and enlargement of Constantine's original decrepit basilica. That prodigious task took more than a century and involved the architectural schemes, first of Bramante, then of Raphael, Sangallo, Michelangelo, della Porta, Fontana and Maderna.

The inimitable splendour and spectacle of St. Peter's Basilica.

St. Peter's is 204 yards long, covering a surface area of more than three and a half acres. Its soaring cupola is 435 feet high with a diameter of 139 feet. Beneath it is Bernini's bronze *baldacchino* (canopy), above the high altar at which only a pope may celebrate mass. Ninety-five lamps burn constantly before the papal **altar,** which is located above the tomb of St. Peter.

Amid the basilica's breathtaking array of gold, mosaic, marble and gilded stucco, the supreme masterpiece is, of course, Michelangelo's **Pietà**. The statue is in the first chapel to the right of the main en-

25

trance. Michelangelo was only 24 when he sculpted this superb marble of the Virgin and the dead Christ, and it was the only work he ever signed—his signature is clearly visible on Mary's sash. Perfectly restored after a hammer attack by a religious fanatic a few years ago, the *Pietà* is now protected by a glass screen and an electronic alarm system.

Before the last pillar on the right near the main altar is the other principal **attraction:** the 13th-century bronze **statue of St. Peter,** by Arnolfo di Cam-

Michelangelo's Pietà—*the artist's only signed work.*

Photo: Mauro Pucciarelli

bio, its foot worn smooth by the kisses of millions of pilgrims.

The basilica contains the reputed wooden chair of St. Peter, enclosed in a baroque sculpture by Bernini. As a magnanimous gesture of reconciliation, Pope Paul VI invited Patriarch Athenagoras I, primate of Eastern Orthodoxy, to sit upon the papal throne at a ceremonial function.

Look *down* as well as up inside St. Peter's. On the floor near the central entrance, a red porphyry disc indicates the spot where Charlemagne knelt to be crowned Holy Roman Emperor in 800. Further along the main aisle towards the altar are markings engraved on the floor, indicating the lengths of the world's other large Catholic churches—any one of which would easily fit in St. Peter's.

To see properly all the art, the crypts and tombs, the sacristy and the basilica's small new museum that replaces the treasury takes at least half a day. St. Peter's is open to the public every day from 7 a.m. until sunset without interruption. Masses are said frequently in the numerous side chapels, at times in languages other than Italian.

The Vatican **grottoes** beneath the basilica, with the tombs of popes John XXIII and Paul VI, close at lunch hour. The pre-Constantinian necropolis, even deeper underground, contains very ancient mausoleums. To visit the necropolis, you must submit a written request to the *Reverenda Fabbrica di San Pietro,* 00120 Vatican City, specifying language spoken, length of visit to Rome, address and telephone number, and then await a reply.

The Vatican Pilgrim and Tourist Information Bureau on St. Peter's Square issues tickets for visits to the grounds of Vatican City, including the magnificent gardens.

In recent years the Vatican has maintained a "decency patrol" at the basilica's entrance. Visitors wearing shorts, barebacked dresses, miniskirts or other scanty attire are politely turned away. During the tourist season, freelance hawkers posted near the statues of saints Peter and Paul on the basilica's porch rent out plastic raincoats to enable over-exposed visitors to get past.

Swiss guards check everyone at the Vatican gates.

Awaiting the pope's balcony appearance in St. Peter's Square.

Though it takes considerable energy and costs several hundred lire, a visit to the top of **St. Peter's dome** is unforgettable. A lift off the left aisle goes as far as the terrace above the nave (if you're walking all the way, it's 537 steps); from there, spiral stairs and ramps lead to the outdoor balcony which circles the top of the dome. The view of Vatican City together with surrounding Rome is spectacular, and there's even an espresso bar.

The Vatican Museum
(Musei Vaticani)

Nothing in all Rome or, quite possibly, the world is as fascinating in its immensity as the palatial maze of more than 1,000 rooms and corridors, known as the Vatican Museum. There are, in fact, eight museums, five galleries, the apostolic library, the Borgia and Raphael rooms and, of course, the Sistine Chapel.

The Vatican Museum is open from 9 a.m. to 2 p.m. (5 p.m. in summer) from Monday to Saturday (except holidays), and it justifiably charges the highest entrance fee in Italy. (On the last Sunday of each month visitors are admitted without charge.)

The entrance on Viale Vaticano is a well signposted 10- or 15-minute walk through the righthand colonnade of St. Peter's Square and on around the Vatican walls.

The use of cameras is normally permitted throughout the museum, but flash bulbs are strictly forbidden in the Sistine Chapel. As at the basilica, improperly attired visitors are turned away. The entire museum complex is protected by closed-circuit television, electronic alarm devices and guards with walkie-talkies.

Below: Raphael at his most sublime. Right: Cool halls of statuary.

THE PICTURE GALLERY
(Pinacoteca Vaticana)

Here, in 15 rooms, are displayed many of the world's most famous paintings, dating back more than 1,000 years to the Byzantine Age. The collection, accumulated by many popes, includes works by Titian, Giotto, Raphael, Caravaggio, Fra Angelico, Leonardo da Vinci, Bellini, Rubens and Van Dyck.

RAPHAEL ROOMS
(Stanze di Raffaello)

Some art lovers spend an entire morning absorbing the masterpieces with which Raphael decorated these four rooms. Don't miss the enormous *Dispute of the Holy Sacrament* and the *School of Athens,* which rank with the very greatest art ever produced. 29

THE SISTINE CHAPEL
(Cappella Sistina)

Probably the most celebrated chamber on earth, this is the private chapel of popes and the site of the secret conclaves at which cardinals elect new popes. The awesome **vaulted** chamber, where total silence is requested of all visitors, is named after Pope Sixtus IV, who ordered it built in the 15th century.

Pinturicchio, with Perugino, Botticelli, Ghirlandaio and Rosselli, covered the chapel's walls with superb frescoes, and then Pope Julius II prevailed on Michelangelo to paint the ceiling. The Florentine genius only reluctantly accepted the monumental task—he was a sculptor, after all.

For more than four years, from 1508 to 1512, working completely alone, Michelangelo advanced swiftly, covering the vast surface in brilliant hues—as the latest astonishing restorations have revealed. And, contrary to legend, he painted erect on tiptoe, craning his neck up—not on his back. When he had finished

The ceiling of the Sistine Chapel is Michelangelo's masterpiece.

portraying the saga of humanity from the Creation to the Flood, he had covered the entire ceiling with the largest painting ever accomplished by a single artist.

Twenty-three years later, when he was more than 60 years old, Michelangelo started the *Last Judgment* on the Sistine's altar wall. That unequalled work, which depicts the end of the world and its rebirth, took seven years.

The overwhelming beauty and power of Michelangelo's achievement can best be appreciated when the Sistine is uncrowded—the wise visitor will walk directly to the chapel through the museum's long corridors as soon as the doors open at 9 a.m. Portable sound-guides are available for hire.

ADDITIONAL SIGHTS

Chapel of Nicholas V *(Cappella di Nicolò V)*. Fra Angelico painted this often overlooked, but exquisite, little chapel in the 15th century.

Pio-Clementine Museum *(Museo Pio-Clementino)*. In the 12 rooms of this museum are housed some of the finest surviving ancient sculptures. Most notable among them are

Laocoön and his sons.

the only copy of the *Venus of Cnidos* by Praxiteles, which is considered the best Greek statue ever done, the massive porphyry fountain from Titus's baths, the statues of the Belvedere *Apollo* and *Mercury,* the *Torso* by Apollonius, and the Rhodean marble group of **Laocoön,** perhaps the greatest treasure in any Vatican museum.

Europe's finest collection of rare books and ancient manuscripts attracts scholars to the Vatican Library (*Biblioteca Vaticana*), where one may see 1,600-year-old copies of Virgil's works, Petrarch's poems, a sixth-century Gospel of St. Matthew, Henry VIII's love letters to Anne Boleyn, and the small medal given to an American Apollo astronaut which he carried to the moon and back.

The infamous Borgias—Caesar, Lucretia and their father, Rodrigo, who became Pope Alexander VI—lived and revelled in the six **Borgia apartments.** Today part of the Vatican's burgeoning new collection of modern religious art is housed in these dazzling rooms.

In the Etruscan Museum (*Museo Etrusco*) you'll see amazing gold jewelry and artefacts found in tombs. There are antique vases and mummies galore in the Egyptian Museum (*Museo Egizio*), more than 5,000 Christian and pagan inscriptions in the Inscription Gallery (*Galleria Lapidaria*), Roman sculpture, sarcophagi and friezes in the Gregorian Profane Museum (*Museo Profano*), fascinating relics from around the world in the Missionary-Ethnological Museum (*Museo Missionario Etnologico*), and carriages and vestments belonging to centuries of popes and cardinals in the Historical Museum (*Museo Storico*).

Classical Rome

The heart of classical Rome comprises the Colosseum, the Forum and environs. Visitors who are particularly interested in ancient Rome will find descriptions of the other major, ancient monuments elsewhere in this book: the Baths of Caracalla (page 41), the Old Appian Way (page 42), the Pantheon (page 55) and Castel Sant'Angelo (page 58).

When planning your sightseeing of this area you may want to include visits to three of Rome's great churches at the same time: St. Peter in Chains, St. Mary Major and St. John Lateran (for descriptions, see pages 66 to 68).

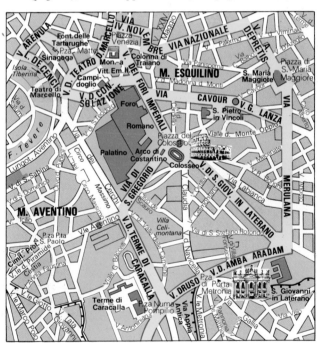

COLOSSEUM
(Colosseo)

Ancient Rome's best known monument, symbolizing the city's continuity through the ages, was the scene of unthinkably brutal spectacles. Built by 20,000 slaves and prisoners, most of them Hebrew, under the Emperor Vespasian and his son Titus, the Colosseum was inaugurated in A.D. 80.

The elliptical arena is surrounded by tiers of stone benches which seated 50,000 people. Through the 80 arched passageways called *vomitoria*, emperors, knights, citizens and slaves thronged in and sat ac-

The Colosseum provides a classical backdrop for newly-weds.

cording to their social status, with the aristocratic élite down closest to the action.

The all-day shows usually began with starving beasts fighting each other: bears, lions, tigers and even elephants were imported from throughout the empire. Then, poorly armed men were turned loose among the animals, and after that, gladiators fought each other to the death as the crowd shouted, *Jugula!* ("Slit his throat"). At other times, the interior was flooded for mock naval battles.

The curious maze of ruins in the arena basin is the Colosseum's substructure of cages, cells and corridors designed to funnel animal and human victims to the slaughter. Doric, Ionic and Corinthian columns support the three arcades. Until the 18th century, popes and princes stripped the Colosseum of much of its marble, travertine and metal to build churches and palaces. Yet, cracking and crumbling, it's the best-preserved ancient amphitheatre anywhere. As the saying goes, "While stands the Colosseum, Rome shall stand; when falls the Colosseum, Rome shall fall; and when Rome falls, with it shall fall the world".

To honour an emperor.

ARCH OF CONSTANTINE
(Arco di Costantino)

Erected next to the Colosseum in A.D. 315 by the Roman Senate, this nearly intact triumphal arch honoured the emperor's victory over pagan Maxentius. It also commemorated the city's conversion to a Christian capital as the result of Constantine's celebrated battlefield vision of the cross. Ironically, most of the reliefs on the arch depict not Constantine but earlier, pagan rulers, because it was built with marble fragments of other ancient monuments, including the arches of Trajan and Marcus Aurelius.

35

ROMAN FORUM
(Foro Romano)

Here echoes the glory that was Rome. Before the emperors, the world had not known a city with a million inhabitants, and on this broad, recessed plain strewn today with frustratingly few marble fragments was the spiritual, political and trading centre of the mighty imperial capital. The Forum was a glittering complex of marble and gold palaces, temples and pillared markets. Sadly, in succeeding centuries barbarian assaults, earthquakes, fires, floods, erosion and plunder by Renaissance architects reduced the area to a muddy cow pasture, its former treasures nearly forgotten. Not until late last century were serious excavations undertaken.

To wander for a few hours through the Forum today is immensely evocative. Open except Tuesday from 9 a.m. (on Sunday 10) until sunset. The hottest hours are best avoided as there's practically no shade. A detailed plan and a portable sound-guide available at the entrance will greatly increase your enjoyment, since the original layout is difficult to conceive.

Part of the **Curia,** where the Roman Senate sat for more than 1,000 years, survives, including its original marble floor. Beneath a protective shed is the famous **Lapis Niger,** a black-marble paving stone installed by Caesar over the presumed site of the grave of Romulus. Here is the oldest Latin inscription ever found, dating back some six centuries before Christ.

Further on are the remnants of the Rostra, the platform for such orators as Cicero and Mark Antony. Only the base columns remain of the Basilica Julia, a law court erected by Caesar; nearby are the three pillars of the Temple of Castor and Pollux, dedicated to those legendary brothers of Helen of Troy.

The well-preserved **Arch of Septimius Severus** was built to honour the emperor who died early in the third century at York *(Eboracum)* in England. Farther away, the **Arch of Titus** with its elaborate bas-reliefs commemorated that emperor's sack of Jerusalem in A.D. 70. Ancient Rome's infamous festival of licentiousness, the Saturnalia, centred on the Temple of Saturn, which was the state treasury until

Caesar looted it during the civil war. Within the circular Temple of Vesta, Rome's sacred flame was kept perpetually lit, guarded by six privileged Vestal Virgins, who were to be buried alive if they transgressed their vow of 30 years of chastity.

Just beyond the Forum lies the **Palatine Hill** *(Palatino)*. This legendary site of Rome's founding is one of the most pleasant places imaginable to have a picnic or simply to sit and look out over the sparse ruins of what was, after the Colosseum, Rome's second

From here Rome ruled the world.

greatest landmark—the Circus Maximus *(Circo Massimo)*. Three hundred years before Christ, a race-course was built here on the reputed site of the Rape of the Sabines. Under the emperors, more than 200,000 citizens would line tiers of marble seats to watch chariots race around the recessed, elongated course. In A.D. 549 after the fall of Rome, Totila the Ostrogoth ended the races, and like so many other magnificent Roman establishments, the Circus Maximus gradually vanished, its marble stripped for the construction of far less glorious edifices.

The nearby imperial forums—named after Trajan, Augustus, Caesar, Vespasian and Domitian—were erected to supplement the Roman Forum as the capital grew ever larger. The most imposing sight in these minor forums is **Trajan's Column,** a remarkably intact monument (138 feet high) erected in A.D. 113. Nineteen huge blocks of marble make up the column topped by a statue of St. Peter, added in the 16th century. Its 850-foot long helicoidal frieze depicts the military victories of the emperor. The 2,500 bas-relief figures on the column show uniforms, weap-

ons, forts, bridges and battles, unfortunately somewhat indistinctly. But the entire frieze is usefully copied at the Museum of Roman Civilization *(Museo di Civiltà Romana)* in the suburban EUR complex (see page 48). Trajan's Forum is closed on Sunday afternoon and all day Monday.

Knights of Malta Square
(Piazza dei Cavalieri di Malta)

Rarely visited by tourists, this delightful, cypress-ringed square on the Aventine *(Aventino)* Hill behind the Circus Maximus features an unexpected telescopic view of St. Peter's dome, slightly more than a mile away. The view is through the peep-hole of a door leading into the spacious private residence of the grand master of the Maltese Knights, a medieval order of knights which aided and protected pilgrims to the Holy Land. Even after you've seen the dome, you don't believe it.

A unique city hall, overlooking Rome from the Capitoline Hill.

CAPITOL SQUARE
(Piazza del Campidoglio)

Crossing over Piazza Venezia (see page 49), you come to Capitol Square.

Michelangelo designed the famous trapezoidal square atop the Capitoline Hill on the most sacred site of ancient Rome, where once sacrifices were made before statues of Jupiter and Juno. Today, the mayor of Rome has his office here in the Senatorial Palace *(Palazzo Senatorio)*.

The bronze statue of the emperor and philosopher Marcus Aurelius, normally in the square, is the only imperial 39

Roman equestrian sculpture in existence. A durable old legend says that the statue is really of gold, covered by a patina, and that when this wears off to reveal the gold, the world will end. Pollution was doing the statue such harm it had to be moved indoors—a chance to diagnose and treat its "illness" before an eventual return.

Since the 13th century, the *Patarina* bell in the Capitoline Tower has been rung only at times of great joy or sorrow for Rome—the annual carnival, a peace treaty, a pope's death, a declaration of war.

In the Palazzo dei Conservatori is kept the hallowed, bronze she-wolf, symbol of the city, superbly sculpted by an Etruscan some six centuries before Christ. However, the twins Romulus and Remus beneath the wolf are not part of the original work but were added during the Renaissance. Until recently, a live wolf was kept caged in the bushes next to Michelangelo's huge stairway leading to the Campidoglio. The smaller, steeper stairs rise to the church of **Santa Maria d'Aracoeli** with its magnificent frescoes, relics and gilded ceiling.

From the Capitol, the view of ancient, Renaissance and modern Rome is particularly striking at sunset.

The Capitoline Picture Gallery displays famous works by Caravaggio, Van Dyck, Velázquez, Titian, Tintoretto, Guercino and Veronese.

Marcus Aurelius on horseback.

Legions of cats prowl the ruins.

Rome's finest public baths. What are now brick walls in the imposing ruins were completely covered with coloured marble; the baths themselves were of alabaster and granite; statuary decorated the bathing rooms and gymnasia; the porticos and ceilings were richly frescoed.

Serving as a meeting place as well as having a hygienic function, Caracalla's luxurious establishment could accommodate 1,600 bathers at a time. The long procedure involved hot and cold baths, steam rooms and rub-downs. The largest hot-bath room, the *calidarium,* is today the stage for Rome's much-admired outdoor opera performances every summer.

Once luxurious baths; now ruins.

BATHS OF CARACALLA
(Terme di Caracalla)

About half a mile south of the Colosseum, for aficionados of classical Rome conveniently in the direction of the Old Appian Way (see page 42), are the Baths of Caracalla.

For 300 years, until barbarians cut the aqueducts in the sixth century, these were

Not all roads led to Rome, but the Appian Way did.

OLD APPIAN WAY
(Via Appia Antica)

To the south of the Baths of Caracalla, at the end of Via di Porta San Sebastiano, begins the Old Appian Way. Though it's inconvenient to visit on a walking tour, you'll find that all travel firms in Rome offer daily guided tours of it by bus. A public bus line runs along some of this ancient southbound route.

When Appius Claudius the Censor* opened it and gave it his name in 312 B.C., this was the grandest road the world had ever known. Over its basalt paving stones, dramatical-

ly visible today outside the city walls, Roman legions rumbled via Capua to Brindisi, where they set sail for the Levant and North Africa.

Flanking this queen of all the Roman consular roads were sepulchres and tombstones of 20 generations of patrician families. Behind the funereal relics today are the walled villas of film celebrities and millionaire aristocrats.

During Nero's frenzied persecution of the Christians, St. Peter was prevailed upon by his followers to leave Rome. Revered tradition records that along the Appian Way he encountered Christ and asked, "Domine, quo vadis?" (Lord, whither goest Thou?). Christ

---

* A magistrate responsible for censuses, who also supervised public morals.

42

replied, "Venio iterum crucifigi" (I come to be crucified again), since Peter was fleeing Rome. Peter turned back to death and martyrdom. The vision vanished, leaving only a footprint. The church of St. Sebastian *(S. Sebastiano),* some one-and-a-half miles out along the Appia, contains a stone reputed to bear that footprint, and a replica is in the nearby Chapel of Quo Vadis marking the site of the remarkable encounter.

Farther along the Appia are the **Catacombs of St. Callistus,** the most important in Rome: a vast underground Christian cemetery notably containing graves of third-century popes. In the Catacombs of St. Sebastian, the bodies of the apostles Peter and Paul are said to have been hidden for decades. In the second and fourth centuries Jews were buried in the Jewish Catacombs, also open to public view along the road.

The cylindrical tomb of Cecilia Metella, a dominating feature of the Appian landscape, was built to commemorate a little-known woman who happened to be related to Crassus, the immensely rich Roman who financed Julius Caesar's early exploits.

The Arch of Drusus at the beginning of the Appia was erected to honour Drusus, nicknamed Germanicus, the first Roman general to reach the North Sea.

Within the catacombs, a statue of St. Cecilia depicts her in death.

Designed to honour the people, the Piazza del Popolo more often provides parking.

The Centre

PIAZZA DEL POPOLO

They also call this aptly named square "The Forum", since everybody who's anybody in present-day Rome meets here.

The piazza is symmetrically perfect, a 150-year-old spatial masterpiece by Valadier, Napoleon's architect. The obelisk in the centre dates from Pharaoh Rameses II, whose glories are hieroglyphically described on all four sides. The twin 17th-century churches of Santa Maria di Monte Santo and Santa Maria de' Miracoli differ only slightly in the shape of their domes.

At the arched gateway begins the Flaminian Way *(Via Flaminia)*, built by Consul Caius Flaminius in 220 B.C., which leads to Rimini on the Adriatic coast. Caravaggio's *Conversion of St. Paul* and *Crucifixion of St. Peter* are among the great paintings displayed in the church of Santa Maria del Popolo.

Just above the piazza is the fountain cascading from the beautiful **garden of the Pincio** with its hundreds of tragically vandalized statues.

Nearby Via Margutta tries gamely to live up to its reputation as one of Europe's great "bohemian" streets: throughout the year outdoor art exhibitions are held here.

45

SPANISH STEPS
(Piazza di Spagna)

The world's most famous steps are really French and Italian, not Spanish. Built early in the 18th century, they ascend via three landings to the major French church in Rome, the twin-belfried Trinità dei Monti. The broad travertine steps are exceptionally beautiful in the spring when they're completely covered with azaleas.

For the rest of the year, the baroque staircase is crowded with lounging youngsters, home-made jewellery vendors and souvenir hawkers.

The endlessly photographed **Trinità dei Monti** above and the adjacent convent belong to the Order of the Sacred Heart and date back 400 years.

To the right of the base of the steps, the house where John Keats died has been preserved as a museum, called the Keats-Shelley Memorial. In the piazza is the 17th-century **Fountain of the Old Boat** *(Fontana della Barcaccia)*, attributed to Pietro Bernini, which supposedly marks the spot where a barge was deposited when the Tiber overflowed its banks.

46   The Spanish embassy to the Holy See is the only Spanish institution now on the square which apparently was named after Spain's embassy to Italy, located here a century ago.

The column rising from the adjacent Piazza Mignanelli, in front of the huge palace of the Vatican's Sacred Congregation for the Evangelization of Peoples, commemorates the Immaculate Conception. Ever since Pope Pius IX proclaimed the dogma of the Immaculate Conception in 1854, popes have made pilgrimages to the monument on December 8th.

On the expensive, fashionable Via Condotti leading directly away from the Spanish Steps, the 200-year-old Caffè Greco boasts of such past customers as Gogol, Goethe, Stendhal, Wagner, Liszt, Byron and E.B. Browning.

The world's smallest state, the Sovereign Military Order of Malta, conducts its charity work from its headquarters at Via Condotti, 68, down the street from Gucci's renowned leather emporium and Bulgari's regal jewellery store.

Smothered in flowers, the Spanish Steps are at their best in spring.

PIAZZA COLONNA

Put up almost exactly 1,800 years ago, the eye-catching column of Marcus Aurelius rises 98 feet above this central square, just in front of the Italian prime-minister's offices in the vast, reddish Chigi Palace *(Palazzo Chigi)*. Two hundred steps lead up to the statue of St. Paul which replaced the original Aurelian bronze in the 16th century. The column's carved reliefs depict the emperor's military triumphs.

On adjacent Parliament Square *(Piazza Montecitorio)*, dominated by the sixth-century B.C. obelisk of the Egyptian Pharaoh Psammetic II, stands the Chamber of Deputies *(Camera dei Deputati)*, Italy's legislative lower house. It was designed by Bernini.

EUR

Mussolini built this suburban complex (just off the Ostia road) of palatial buildings, miniature lakes and arenas for a world's fair washed out by the war. Now primarily a commercial and residential area, EUR (for *Esposizione Universale Roma)*, is worth visiting to see Nervi's celebrated sports palace *(Palazzo dello Sport)*, and the Museum of Roman Civilization *(Museo della Civiltà Romana)*, which has an outstanding model of ancient Rome and reproductions of some of imperial Rome's greatest treasures. Children delight in EUR's fun fair.

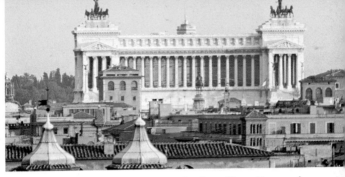

Turn-of-the-century monument to Italy's first king, Victor Emmanuel.

From Piazza Colonna you can either window-shop your way along Via del Corso to Piazza Venezia or get a quick glimpse of the old town near the Pantheon (see page 55) and look in at the famous Church of the Jesus (see page 69).

PIAZZA VENEZIA

However hard one may try, it's impossible to avoid this huge, traffic-jammed square which is considered the centre of modern Rome. The white-marble Victor Emmanuel monument towering over the square was aptly nicknamed the "wedding cake" by World War II British soldiers. Romans sneer at it as an architectural monstrosity; visitors gawk and climb to the top for a splendid panoramic view. Built between 1885 and 1911 to honour the unification of Italy and her first king, the monument contains the Tomb of the Unknown Soldier beneath the royal equestrian statue, along with garish representations of the motherland and military valour.

In stunning contrast, the 15th-century **Palazzo Venezia** along one side of the same square has been called the finest palace ever built in Christian Rome. Now a museum of Renaissance art (open every morning except Monday), the palace was a papal home, the embassy of the Republic of Venice and later Mussolini's official residence. From its tiny central balcony, *il Duce* delivered his major speeches. 49

Changing of the guard at the presidential palace.

QUIRINAL PALACE
(Palazzo del Quirinale)

The presidents of Italy normally live in this immense palace which has rooms enough to house a regiment. Under construction for two centuries starting in 1574, the Quirinal was the residence of many popes during a long period when malarial vapours stalked the swampy Vatican area across the Tiber.

In the Quirinal's 18th-century Pauline Chapel *(Cappella Paolina)*, whose dimensions are exactly the same as those of the Sistine Chapel, conclaves to choose popes were held until 1870. Italian kings then moved in. Since the last war, Italy's chiefs of state have entertained top foreign dignitaries here. Special permission may be obtained through the Rome tourist board to get past the towering palace guards.

Every summer, the president holds Rome's most lavish outdoor reception in the vast and magnificently manicured Quirinal gardens. The palace is named after and built on the Hill of Quirinus (the ancient Sabine name for the god Mars), one of Rome's original seven hills. From the piazza, bearing the same name as the palace, with its famous statue of Castor and Pollux, is one of the best panoramic views of Rome and Vatican City.

TREVI FOUNTAIN
(Fontana di Trevi)

After Nicola Salvi sculpted this huge baroque fountain in the 18th century, the superstition was that a traveller who drank its "virgin water" *(acqua vergine)* would be sure to come back to Rome. Nowadays, to achieve the same assurance, you turn your back and toss a coin over your shoulder into the basin.

Every day some 20 million gallons of Rome's most prized water (it's softer at least) pour through the Trevi's extravagant waterscape. It comes from a spring discov-

Tourists toss coins to say, "Arrivederci, Roma".

Bright lights and cafés attract thousands to Via Veneto.

ered by a virtuous maiden 13 miles from Rome in the days of the imperial legions, and it's transported over an aqueduct built by Marcus Agrippa in 19 B.C. to this and several other fountains in the town.

Traffic has now been banned from the small square in front of this landmark, but it's usually very crowded, making photography or coin-throwing difficult. Like so many Roman monuments, the Trevi is vastly more impressive at night when it's floodlit. By then, with the crowds thinned, the romance of the fountain regains sway.

On certain mornings you may see hordes of small boys dodging past policemen to snatch coins as the basin is emptied for cleaning. Authori-

ties take a dim view of this, since the considerable revenue tossed into the water should be the property of the bankrupt city of Rome.

VIA VENETO

This best-known of Roman thoroughfares is still a smart promenade during the daytime, but is not recommended at night. The shops, hotels and cafés are sometimes elegant, often fashionable, but always expensive. Take a seat at an open-air café, and while you sit and sip your refreshing *granita di caffè,* you can watch all the beautiful and not-so-beautiful people go by. Chances are they won't be Romans but fellow tourists.

BORGHESE GALLERY
(Galleria Borghese)

No art lover should miss this small but absolutely outstanding collection of masterpieces, displayed in a pavilion within the beautiful Borghese Park *(Villa Borghese)*. Here are Raphael's *Deposition from the Cross,* Titian's *Sacred and Profane Love,* and the young Bernini's stunning sculptures of *David* and *Apollo and Daphne,* along with famous works by such masters as Rubens, Correggio, Veronese, Botticelli and Caravaggio. Open every morning except Monday, the Borghese can be enjoyed at leisure in perhaps two hours. A walk through the peaceful surrounding Borghese gardens, past lakes, a waterclock and numerous statues, provides delightful relief from the noisy frenzy of the big city.

Note: The Italian State Tourist Office (see p. 122) issues student-rate passes for museums, art galleries and monuments on presentation of student identification.

From floor to ceiling the Borghese Gallery offers a breathtaking display of Italian masterpieces.

⚔ Old Rome*

To stroll through the twisting, cobblestoned streets around Piazza Navona, the Pantheon and Campo de' Fiori is to journey backwards in time. In this quarter with palaces, courtyard fountains and churches, the "feel" of Rome as it was centuries ago still lingers.

And be sure to take your camera to this truly picturesque, Roman Rome. Carpenters craft instant antiques in musty cellars; tiger kittens snooze in the sun on top of Fiats parked in tiny squares; a wine merchant taps a barrel and pours drinks all around.

* Chronologically speaking, "old Rome" might more accurately be called Medieval Rome. This section includes other nearby attractions you may want to visit while in "old Rome".

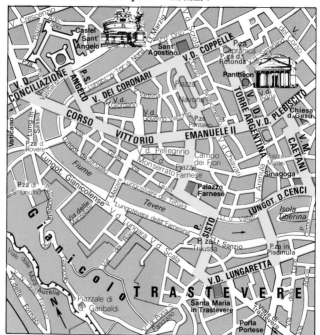

PANTHEON

Consul Marcus Agrippa first built this astonishing "temple of all the gods" almost exactly 2,000 years ago–in 27 B.C. In the second century Hadrian reconstructed it, after a disastrous fire in 80 A.D., in the form which survives today. It became a church in the 7th century. Known also as the *Rotonda*, the Pantheon features a majestic dome with a diameter (142 feet) identical to its height, a triumph of architectural harmony.

Each of the 16 massive, reddish-grey columns supporting the portico is made from a single piece of Egyptian granite. The original bronze doors, still intact, weigh 20 tons. Ten times that much bronze was stripped from the ceiling in the 17th century by Pope Urban VIII and used, it's said, to decorate St. Peter's. Every bit of the marble which once covered the walls was plundered.

The Pantheon is open daily from 9 a.m. to sunset. It's best to visit when the sun is high in the sky—the vault's only light comes through the opening in the dome which measures 30 feet in diameter. Curiously, few of the statues or paintings in this majestic temple are of major importance. But in side chapels are the tombs of the artist Raphael and the first two kings of united Italy, Victor Emmanuel II and Umberto I. You can see the Pantheon in 15 minutes; you're likely to remember it for a lifetime.

A halo of light illuminates the interior of the Pantheon.

Pedestrians and pigeons share the piazza.

PIAZZA NAVONA

Romans insist fondly that this is the most beautiful square in the world, and it's very easy to agree. Piazza Navona covers the site of the first-century A.D. Stadium of Domitian, retaining its exact rectangular dimensions (787 by 213 feet). Sporting events were held here, and in later centuries the square was often flooded so that noble families could amuse themselves in the artificial lake.

Thanks to an enlightened recent decision of Roman authorities, the square has been declared a pedestrian-only zone *(isola pedonale)*. As a result, there's no more pleasant place in the city for an outdoor meal or drink, allowing time for a leisurely study of Bernini's famous **Fountain of the Four Rivers** in the centre of the square. The figures gushing water beneath the obelisk represent the Nile, Ganges, de la Plata and Danube. Bernini sculpted the magnificent baroque fountain in 1654, a few years before his great rival architect, Borromini, constructed the church of St. Agnes *(Santa Agnese)* a few yards away. These dates should disprove—but don't—the persistent Roman legend that Bernini was so scornful of Borromini's talents that he made one figure with an arm stretched out toward the church, as if to guard against its inevitable collapse.

The majestic power of Bernini.

In December, the square is jammed with booths for the hugely colourful Christmas and Epiphany *(Befana)* Fair.

Italy's senate convenes in Palazzo Madama, named after Margaret of Austria, the illegitimate daughter of Emperor Charles V. On the adjacent Piazza S. Eustachio is the bar which Romans say serves the best coffee in the city.

The 15th-century church of S. Agostino, built from travertine blocks ripped off the Colosseum, was the church of Rome's most renowned Renaissance courtesans, devout beauties who entertained the cream of society in their Old Rome salons nearby. Such artistic giants as Raphael also worshipped here.

Renaissance flavour is delightfully preserved in **Via dei Coronari** (Street of the Rosary-makers), Rome's most famous street of antique shops. It's pricey, and many pieces are in fact imported from London, but collectors flock here from around the world. Along Via dei Coronari is the huge and sombre Lancellotti Palace *(Palazzo Lancellotti)*, seat of a great aristocratic family. In 1870 when Italian troops occupied papal Rome, the prince was so angered that he locked his main door, and it wasn't reopened until the 1929 Lateran Pact reconciled church and state. Close by in the towering church of **S. Salvatore in Lauro** is what many artists consider the most architecturally perfect little cloister in Rome.

Once a mausoleum, a fortress and a prison, now an impressive museum.

CASTEL SANT'ANGELO

Hadrian built this grim and stoutly circular landmark on the opposite bank of the Tiber more than 1,800 years ago as his imperial mausoleum. Most of its original grandeur disappeared, for it was soon converted into a fortress which remained Rome's mightiest military bastion for centuries. Popes fled to safety from assorted invaders along the thick-walled passage connecting St. Peter's with the castle. Here they kept the Vatican's most precious possessions in treasure chests which are still on view.

During the last sack of Rome, in 1527, Pope Clement VII was besieged for a month but held out high inside the turreted fortress, watching helplessly as the German and Spanish mutineers ravaged his city (see page 15).

Castel Sant'Angelo is best known as a dreadful prison, which it remained from the Renaissance until the beginning of this century. Off the spiral ramp are cells which held scores of famous prisoners. At least one cardinal was strangled here; other inmates were hanged from the battlements.

The castle takes its name from Pope Gregory's miraculous vision in 590 of an angel alighting on its turret, whereupon a plague decimating Rome suddenly vanished. Today a marble angel by Giacomo della Porta is on display in one of the courtyards.

Visitors may hire portable sound-guides which describe in any of five languages the fascinating military implements and Renaissance furnishings on view in the fortress-museum. Castel Sant'Angelo is open every morning and some afternoons except Monday when it is closed all day.

FARNESE PALACE
(Palazzo Farnese)

Since the fortunate French maintain their embassy here, tourists are admitted to the grounds of this superb Renaissance palace for only one hour a week, between 11 a.m. and noon on Sunday. In the 16th century, it took the renowned artists, Antonio Sangallo, Michelangelo and Giacomo della Porta, more than 50 years to build the palace. Michelangelo did the spectacular cornice and the top floor, the central window of the façade and part of the courtyard on commission from the owner, the rich Prince Alessandro Farnese. This Renaissance nobleman had four children by a mistress while he was a cardinal. Later he reformed and became Pope Paul III. His collection of marble statuary is superb.

Piazza Farnese has been turned into one of Rome's few traffic-free squares; at night the only sound you hear is the water splashing into the Egyptian granite basins of the famous twin Farnese fountains.

The area between the Sant'Angelo Bridge *(Ponte Sant'Angelo)* and the Farnese 59

Despite supermarkets, produce stands draw daily shoppers.

Palace is full of evocative, narrow streets that are a joy in themselves.

Look for Via dei Cappellari (Street of the Hat-makers), Via dei Balestrari (Crossbow makers), Via dei Chiavari (Locksmiths), Via del Pellegrino—where Holy-Year pilgrims used to pass on their way to St. Peter's. On Via di Monserrato is the Venerable English College, dating from 1362, the oldest English institution abroad. The Palazzo della Cancelleria is where three exiled British Stuarts lived in the 18th century, and where, in 1969, five new American cardinals-designate sat awaiting Vatican messengers bearing their red berets.

CAMPO DE' FIORI

For a marvellously entertaining glimpse of the Romans being Roman, don't miss gay and bustling Campo de' Fiori. Oddly enough, the city's best and busiest outdoor market is located on a site long notorious for its public executions. The statue rising above the maze of fruit, vegetable, fish, meat and flower stalls is of Giordano Bruno, a philosopher burned alive here as a heretic on February 17, 1600. Some years later, two monks were executed on the same spot for scheming to end the life of Pope Urban VIII through black magic.

Every morning except Sunday, housewives haggle over

tomatoes and tripe, vendors sing out their bargains, and everybody loudly admires everybody else's baby. In the afternoon, after the umbrellas and stands are taken down, young political militants or Rome's active women's liberation movement may fill the square for protest demonstrations—building bonfires from artichoke husks or orange crates. Some of the ordinary-looking cafés adjoining the square are said to be hangouts of the city's underworld.

A few steps from Campo de' Fiori beneath little Piazza del Biscione was Pompey's Theatre, where Julius Caesar fell dead of 23 dagger wounds inflicted by such trusted associates as Brùtus. Thereafter, Marc Antony trotted over to the Forum for his famous oration. A restaurant called *Pancrazio* today marks the long-buried assassination site.

The 17th-century church of S. Andrea della Valle, with the city's second tallest dome after St. Peter's, is the setting for the first act of *Tosca*. The church was built over a period of 60 years, the work of three different architects. Inside there are impressive statues and frescoes.

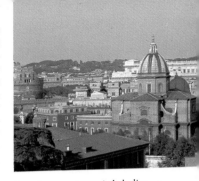

Rome's many-centuried skyline.

THE JANICULUM HILL
(Gianicolo)

For a picnic, a shaded stroll or the best panoramic view of Rome and the surrounding green countryside, the Janiculum Hill is the spot. Here Garibaldi's forces (see HISTORY) fought one of their fiercest battles, and the hero's equestrian statue commemorates it. Nearby is a "lighthouse" donated by Italians living in Argentina. On the slopes of the Janiculum, so named because the Roman god Janus was once worshipped here, is the Roman Catholic seminary called the North American College. It has been the training ground for many American and Canadian prelates.

61

A Roman favourite: the Fountain of the Tortoises.

THE GHETTO

Jews have lived in Rome since the 5th century B.C., confined and persecuted for vastly more of the time than they were left alone. In the 16th century, Pope Paul IV ordered them into the ghetto area. Except for brief freedom under Napoleon, Jews were forbidden until 1870 to practise professions, own land or hold public office, and were forced to wear a yellow skull-cap to distinguish them. Dominating the ghetto, which survives much less grimly today, is the Portico d'Ottavia, a crumbling, arched façade more than 2,000 years old. This marked the entrance area to the adjacent Theatre of Marcellus *(Teatro di Marcello)* begun by Caesar, which held over 10,000 spectators.

Today, Jews live in all sections of Rome, but despite past memories, the picturesque ghetto along the Tiber, with its Assyro-Babylonian synagogue and Jewish museum (open daily except Saturday), remains the most characteristic area. Some of Rome's best restaurants and shopping bargains are found in this bustling quarter, and in recent years a new flavour has been added by scores of Jewish emigrants from the Soviet Union.

Probably the most delightful fountain in Rome, the 16th-century **Fountain of the Tortoises** *(Fontana delle Tartarughe)* in Piazza Mattei, is the ghetto's best-loved landmark.

TRASTEVERE

Always crowded, noisy and cheerful, this ancient Roman quarter with its mystifying maze of cobblestoned streets is the most popular in the city today. Trastevere (the name means "across the Tiber") lives outdoors about eight months a year. The district has only one hotel, which is no tragedy—silence never descends before the early hours of the morning, if at all.

The sharp-tongued Trasteverini claim (incorrectly) that they're the only true descendants of the ancient Romans or Etruscans, people quite apart from those "foreigners" across the river who speak the language with such a curious accent. In fact, you may still find a few Trasteverini who swear they've never been across the Tiber.

In July the district stages a marvellous outdoor festival called *Noiantri* (meaning "we

Traffic noise doesn't discourage a strolling accordionist.

The ancient, serene beauty of Santa Maria in Trastevere. Right:
Beautiful, 13th-century cloister provides a peaceful oasis.

others'' in their dialect) with
fireworks, minstrel music and
street games—the most colourful festival in Rome.

Trastevere surrounds imp-
ressive **Santa Maria in Trastevere,** believed to be Rome's
oldest church, fronting onto
the popular and traffic-free
piazza of the same name. The
basilica was built by Pope Callistus I in the 3rd century A.D.,
on the spot where legend
says oil gushed from the earth
to presage the birth of Christ.
The façade's 13th-century gild-

ed mosaics, thoughtfully illu-
minated at night, attract
droves of tourists and even Roman jet-setters to the piazza's
cafés and restaurants.

In nearby Piazza San Cosi-
mato, a wonderful fruit and
vegetable market operates every morning except Sunday.
Aside from some of Rome's
most charming courtyards,
alleyways and old houses,
wandering through Trastevere
you'll come upon the city's jail,
called *Regina Coeli* (Queen of
Heaven).

The Churches of Rome

Even if you never go near a church, Rome's the place to make an exception. A brief visit allows time to see only a handful of the city's 500 churches; in addition to St. Peter's (see page 24), most tourists will want to visit Rome's three other magnificent patriarchal basilicas and at least two other famous churches.

THE BASILICA OF ST. PAUL'S OUTSIDE THE WALLS
(San Paolo fuori le Mura)

On the way to St. Paul's you can pass the peacefully beautiful Protestant Cemetery (Cimitero Protestante), near Porta San Paolo, where Keats is buried and Shelley's ashes are interred.

Looming over the graves is the striking, white, 131-foot pyramid of Gaius Cestius, which was erected as that Roman praetor's* tomb in 12 B.C. St. Paul is thought to have been led through the Aurelian gate down the Ostian Way (Via Ostiense) to his execution where his basilica now stands.

This basilica, the largest in Rome after St. Peter's, was originally built by Constantine in 315 and later enlarged by Valentinian and Theodosius. It survived, astonishingly, until a tragic fire in 1823, whereafter it was faithfully restored with contributions from around the world. The enormously impressive interior has 86 Venetian marble columns and above them, beneath the alabaster windows, runs a row of mosaic medallions representing all the popes since Peter.

---

* An annually elected magistrate in ancient Rome.

Under the canopied altar the presumed remains of St. Paul are kept in a marble urn. The paschal candle by the 12th-century artist Pietro Vassalletto is the world's largest; his strikingly beautiful **cloister,** which was somehow undamaged in the great fire, is Rome's finest. The Benedictine monks who live and make jewellery and liqueurs at St. Paul's shuffle along the corridors in their flowing robes.

The devout climb the Holy Steps.

THE BASILICA OF ST. JOHN LATERAN
(San Giovanni in Laterano)

Devoutly regarded as the mother cathedral of the Catholic world (it's the seat of the pope as Bishop of Rome), the original Lateran predates St. Peter's. It was also built by Constantine in the 4th century. Popes lived here for a thousand years. On the wooden altar preserved in the basilica's sanctuary, St. Peter is believed to have celebrated mass.

Fires, vandals and earthquakes ruined the Lateran through the centuries. The current basilica, less than 300 years old, is at least the fifth on this site.

Facing the basilica is the ancient edifice that houses the Scala Santa, the holy stairway which, according to tradition, Jesus trod in the house of Pontius Pilate. The 28 marble steps may be ascended only on one's knees.* The Egyptian obelisk in the Lateran square, 148 feet high, is the oldest of the 13 now standing in Rome and the tallest in the world. It was originally erected at the Temple of Ammon in Thebes in 1449 B.C.

---

* An Augustinian monk, Martin Luther, also once ascended these steps on his knees. Even today, saying the rosary on these hallowed steps is believed to release a soul from purgatory.

THE BASILICA OF ST. MARY MAJOR
(Santa Maria Maggiore)

A pilgrim's favourite for centuries, the world's largest church dedicated to the Virgin Mary is practically unchanged since it was built on the Esquiline *(Esquilino)* Hill more than 1,500 years ago. Its treasures are dazzling: the incomparably rich Pauline Chapel *(Cappella Paolina)* has an altar of lapis lazuli, amethyst and agate with a revered painting of the

A cross tops an Egyptian obelisk.

Obelisks

When Napoleon jokingly asked Canova if Romans knew how to plant trees, the sculptor replied, "Trees, your Majesty? In Rome they plant obelisks". During the Caesarian empire, 48 of these stone spires stood in Rome, all transported as booty from the Nile Valley. Today 13 still stand, most of them repaired and moved to their present sites by past popes, who presumably overlooked their obvious symbolic significance.

Madonna and Child dating back perhaps 1,200 years. Every August 5, white flower petals are showered down onto the altar to mark the date when, according to still another beloved legend, snow miraculously fell on this spot as the Virgin had told Pope Liberius it would.

The basilica also claims to contain the wood and metal relics of the holy crib, which can be seen on the 25th day of each month. They are venerated in a glittering ceremony on Christmas Eve. Julian Sangallo decorated Santa Maria's 67 ceiling in the 16th century with the first gold ever brought from America.

Forty Ionic columns divide the basilica's triple nave. Above the columns are scenes from the Old Testament, depicted in 36 mosaic panels about 1,500 years old.

Michelangelo's Moses.

ST. PETER IN CHAINS
(San Pietro in Vincoli)

The Empress Eudossia founded the church in the fifth century as the sanctuary for the chains with which Herod bound St. Peter in Palestine. These chains, and others used on Peter when he was imprisoned in Rome, are kept in a bronze reliquary under the high altar. The original church was rebuilt in the 15th century and then was restored during the 18th century.

Majestically seated on the tomb of Pope Julius II is Michelangelo's **statue of Moses,** considered by some to be the sculptor's greatest work. For better viewing and photography, a coin-operated device lights up the magnificent creation done from a single piece of white Carrara marble.

It's popularly believed that the small gash in Moses' knee was caused when Michelangelo hurled his hammer at the stunningly lifelike statue and commanded it to speak.

Unfortunately, droves of souvenir hawkers and freelance guides besiege the huge crowds at this tourist favourite, but seeing the *Moses* is worth any discomfort.

CHURCH OF THE JESUS
(Il Gesù)

Few churches in the world are as overpowering as this, the mother church of the Roman Catholic order of Jesuits. Built **four centuries ago**, *il Gesù* is literally awash in glittering gold, semi-precious stones and mosaics. Its richness eloquently attests to the power and prestige of the famous order.

St. Ignatius of Loyola, founder of the Company of Jesus, is entombed in the left transept under the largest piece of lapis lazuli in existence. Coin-operated sound guides describe the interior to visitors.

Dazzling riches and a stern tradition—Il Gesù, mother church of the Jesuits.

Excursions

POMPEII

High on every list of the wonders of the world, the remarkable ruins of Pompeii await the visitor just a three-hour bus or car ride south of Rome along the picturesque Highway of the Sun (*Autostrada del Sole*). Ancient Pompeii, which is still being excavated, sprawls at the foot of Mount Vesuvius overlooking the Bay of Naples, an unforgettable start to a one- or two-day excursion for tourists based in the capital.

Founded some seven centuries before Christ where the fertile Sarno Valley sweeps towards the sea, Pompeii became a prosperous Roman colony in 80 B.C. Its 20,000 inhabitants built impressive temples, forums and villas with the income from a thriving agricultural commerce. In those days the slopes of Vesuvius were covered with vineyards and wooded groves, a pleasant and—it was thought—benign mountainous backdrop for the bustling town.

Then, in A.D. 79, Vesuvius suddenly revealed itself as a volcano, erupting with colossal force. Pompeii was buried by more than 20 feet of volcanic ash, lava and rock, many of the estimated 2,000 victims overcome by poisonous gases as they tried to flee.

The site was never again inhabited and, in fact, Pompeii was all but forgotten until ex-

Tourists inspect the site where lava and ash smothered a city.

cavations began in the 18th century.

To walk the cobbled Roman-era streets of Pompeii today is to experience the uncanny feeling of actually being there when the catastrophe struck. Archaeologists have reconstructed casts of Pompeiian bodies frantically trying to escape the fumes. Household implements have been unearthed just as they were on that fateful day 1,900 years ago. Wall frescoes, statuary and jewelry are still being uncovered by excavators, striking evidence of a wealthy and contented society suddenly and totally snuffed out.

The best way to appreciate Pompeii is to engage one of the experienced and multilingual guides at the entrance. He'll lead you through the streets showing you the efficient Roman sewer system (something nearby Naples lacks to this day), past mills, shops and public baths, to the **forum** where Pompeians convened for political and religious events, to the strikingly beautiful villas of the richest merchants, and on to the first-century B.C. amphitheatre with seats for 20,000 spectators, the oldest extant Roman theatre. A guide will also be able to arrange entrance to some displays of colourfully erotic Pompeian art not open to general view.

No one will want to spend less than three or four hours wandering through the marvellously preserved ruins, which 71 offer countless photographic attractions. At Pompeii you'll find a museum housing many of the excavated treasures, the rest being on view at the National Museum *(Museo Nazionale)* in Naples 15 miles away. A restaurant and snack bar are conveniently located next to the museum.

Not far from Pompeii there's a chair lift up to the rim of Vesuvius's 3,890-foot high crater, offering a view not only of the menacing "Valley of Hell", but a glorious panorama of Naples and the entire bay area. Also close at hand is the smaller excavated site of the town of Herculaneum, buried by the same A.D. 79 eruption of that still occasionally rumbling volcano.

An alternative way to reach Pompeii is by train from Rome to Naples and then bus or taxi.

CAPRI

From either Naples or Sorrento, it's an easy motor-boat *(vaporetto)* or hydrofoil *(aliscafo)* trip out to Capri, the fabled green isle of the Parthenopean Gulf. Brushing past the legions of souvenir hawkers awaiting incoming tourists, one should locate the excursion boats which circle the island in 90 minutes and include a stop, calm sea permitting, at the Blue Grotto *(Grotta Azzurra)*. In this spectacular limestone sea cave, the reflections on the water create an eerily beautiful iridescence which countless artists and poets have laboured to capture.

From the harbour a funicular railway goes up to the colourful town of Capri. On a brief visit to the island, one should at least see the **Villa Jovis,** the hilltop holiday palace of the Roman Emperor Tiberius. Nearby is the high rocky precipice called "Tiberius's Leap"—where the emperor amused himself by having his enemies or playmates who displeased him cast off into the sea.

Before you leave the island, you may be surprised to learn that it's properly pronounced *Ca*pri, with the first syllable accented, despite the well-known song about the isle of Ca*pree.*

AMALFI DRIVE

Half an hour along the coast from Pompeii at Sorrento begins the Amalfi Drive *(Strada Panoramica Amalfitana),* often called Europe's most beautiful coast road. Featuring twisting, hairpin bends along a breathtakingly rugged coast, grottoes, olive and lemon groves and an inviting view of Capri, the Amalfi Drive winds on for about 30 miles to the busy seaport of Salerno.*

On this spectacular coastal road, most popular stop-over is **Positano.** Pink, white and yellow houses and hotels perch dramatically on the steep hillsides of a magnificent ravine which plunges to the sea. Bougainvillea abounds; the scent of orange blossoms overwhelms. Restaurants specialize in fresh seafood but serve pizza and the other familiar Neapolitan dishes as well. At Positano's several dozen hotels and boarding-houses, there's almost always someone who speaks English. For breakfast or tea, don't miss the Positano sugar doughnuts (ciambelli).

Farther south lies Amalfi, a once-thriving port city which gives its name to the coastal road. Today a somewhat commercialized resort, Amalfi was Italy's oldest sea republic.

Smaller but always picturesque villages, some with pleas-

A perilous drive of unmatched beauty.

ant bathing beaches, are found all the way to Salerno. Here the motorist can pick up the autostrada which heads back north directly to Rome, a drive of perhaps four to five hours. 73

* Scene of an Allied landing in 1943 which hastened the liberation of Italy.

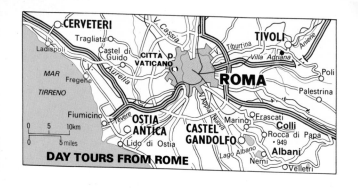

DAY TOURS FROM ROME

THE ALBAN HILLS AND CASTEL GANDOLFO

Better—if imprecisely—known as the *Castelli Romani* ("Roman Castles"), the charming Alban Hill towns are easily reached from Rome along the southbound New Appian Way *(Via Appia Nuova)*. The trip makes an ideal half-day excursion. Vineyards on the slopes above Lake Albano and Lake Nemi produce most of the white wine drunk in Rome, and such villages as Marino, Rocca di Papa and Frascati are famous for their grape-harvest festivals in the autumn. For nature lovers and seekers of rural Italian atmosphere, this is ideal territory.

In the wooded hills there are ruined castles to explore, panoramas over deep, blue lakes and friendly townspeople who delight in sharing a glass of wine straight from the barrel with visitors.

At various times throughout the year, the little villages stage dramatic religious festivals—try to plan your trip to coincide with one.

For most tourists, **Castel Gandolfo** is the prime attraction of the Alban Hills *(Colli Albani)*. Here, since the 17th century, has stood the summer palace of the popes, regally overlooking Lake Albano. The pope is in residence at Castel Gandolfo from mid-July until early September, fleeing

74

Rome at its hottest period. With a reduced work schedule, he relaxes amid some of the most beautifully landscaped gardens in the world. On Sundays at noon, the pope addresses and blesses the thousands of pilgrims who flock to the small village which thrives primarily on souvenir sales.

The palace, gardens and Vatican observatory on the grounds are only rarely open to visitors and never while the pope is staying here. Special buses take tourists to the summer papal audiences from Rome, and Castel Gandolfo is included on all the many guided excursions to the Alban Hills offered by Rome travel agencies. There are also city buses serving the hill towns. But the best way to see and enjoy the area is by hired car, which would permit a picnic or a meal at one of the many outdoor *trattorie*.

TIVOLI

For a delightful change of pace from the sights and sounds of Rome, visitors for centuries have travelled 19 miles eastward along the Tiburtine Way

The papal observatory.

(*Via Tiburtina*) to Tivoli. Here, on rolling hills commanding a view of the vast Roman plain, the Emperor Hadrian, architect of Rome's Pantheon, the **famous wall in England and much else**, built what is surely one of the largest and most elaborate retirement hideaways ever devised.

Known as **Hadrian's Villa (*Villa Adriana*)**, it covers 173 acres and evokes the emperor's favourite sights during his world travels in the second century A.D. Temples, baths, bridges, fountains, marble columns and entire, reconstructed valleys and canals are found in various states of preservation throughout the immense estate. Hadrian intended it as 75

Not everyone has a washing-machine.

the consummate pleasure palace for a long retirement, but he survived for only a few years. In succeeding centuries its manifold art treasures were looted; today some are on view in various Italian and foreign museums.

Just as compelling is the **Villa D'Este** in the town of Tivoli itself. Conceived by the 16th-century cardinal Ippolito d'Este, this Renaissance residence is surrounded by a garden wonderland featuring 500 fountains and countless beautiful optical illusions, created from cascading water, reflecting pools and artfully placed trees.

Tivoli is well advertised as a half-day excursion by Rome's travel agencies. Some trips include a meal stop. A city bus line operates on the same route. With traffic it's about a 75-minute trip in either direction. Part of the year, Tivoli's sights are closed on Monday.

OSTIA ANTICA

Excavations are still uncovering other fascinating sections of what was once the seaport of ancient Rome, a long-buried city 14 miles from the capital on the shores of the Tyrrhenian Sea. This is an interesting half-day excursion for archaeology fans.

Ocean vessels were unable to proceed inland along the shallow Tiber, so the inhabitants of Ostia trans-shipped the imperial booty to river barges and sent them off to Rome. In its palmiest days, Ostia had 100,000 residents and boasted splendid baths, temples, a theatre and imposing houses.

Both guides and descriptive brochures are available. The well-preserved ruins are set among lovely pine forests on the coastal plain. The modern seaside resort of Ostia, nearby, is tremendously popular with

Romans; dinner at open-air restaurants is very pleasant, but swimming is not (see p. 94).

Rome's metro runs to Ostia, as do city buses and guided excursions. The trip takes about 45 minutes. Or go by boat in summer from Ponte Marconi.

World War II veterans and enthusiasts of military history might wish to travel 25 miles south from Ostia along the coast to Anzio and Nettuno, scene of the bitter fighting surrounding the Allied landings in 1944, now the site of British and American cemeteries.

Ostia's pillars and pines.

CERVETERI

For archaeology lovers or those whose appetites have been whetted in Rome museums, there's an intriguing experience 27 miles north along the coast around the town of Cerveteri. Here, on the site of one of the original 12 towns of the Etruscan League, are scores of shaft-tombs of those powerful and mysterious pre-Christian people who produced such amazingly refined jewellery. Guides escort visitors into the tombs and describe the impressive Banditaccia Necropolis *(Necropoli di Banditaccia).*

"Genuine" artefacts offered for sale by street vendors are best avoided: gifted fabricators abound locally. But professional collectors, through careful inquires, may find some authentic pieces. These cannot, however, be exported from Italy without official permission (see CUSTOMS AND ENTRY REGULATIONS). Prices for the beautiful vases, necklaces and amulets having soared on the world market in recent years, tomb looters are still discovering and pillaging graves in this area.

Guided tours to Cerveteri and nearby Etruscan sites may be arranged through some Rome travel firms, and public buses also operate daily.

Boutiques display luxury items. Right: *Street stands offer bargains.*

Shopping

Rome's international reputation as a marvellous shopping city is unquestionably deserved. All those famous Italian high-fashion brands are on sale at prices often far lower than abroad. And nowhere is the Italian flair for display more striking than in the shop windows with their varied and tasteful offerings. It takes willpower indeed not to succumb, as countless tourists have discovered.

Here are some basic recommendations for shopping in Rome:

Worth buying

Leather: gloves, shoes, jackets, bags, belts, wallets, desk sets, luggage.

Silk: blouses, shirts, dresses, suits, scarves, ties.

Knitwear, ceramics, costume jewelry, Italian art and antiques, straw goods (but Florence is better), and Italian wine and spirits.

Worth avoiding

Cameras, radios, tape recorders, gold (Florence is far better), toys, non-Italian books, tobacco products, foreign perfumes, Italianate foreign antiques.

Where to shop

Rome's most fashionable shopping district is found between the Spanish Steps and Via del Corso, notably including Via Condotti, Via Frattina and Via Borgognona. Some of Europe's finest shops and boutiques are here, but while bargains can occasionally be found, smart Roman shoppers go elsewhere —and pay considerably less.

A favoured "secret" shopping street is the long and perfectly obvious **Via Cola di Rienzo** across the Tiber. Prices are also more reasonable along **Via Nazionale** and in the twisting old Rome streets near Campo de' Fiori and the Pantheon. For shopping and everything else, economy-conscious Romans assiduously avoid the appallingly expensive Via Veneto area. The city's few (and small) department stores offer good buys and, though crowded, are a colourful delight to wander through. The *Saldi* signs often posted mean sales.

When to shop

By 8.30 or 9 a.m. at the latest, Rome's shops are open for business. Many close for siesta between 1 and 3.30 p.m., and then reopen until 7.30 or 8 p.m., but most of the large stores are open nonstop and many of the smaller ones in the centre are following suit. In summer most shops close on Saturday afternoon, in winter, on Monday morning (except groceries, which close on Thursday afternoons).

Markets

Called Porta Portese, Rome's incredible **flea market** extends for about 2½ miles of avenues, streets and alleys. It begins at a battered archway—the Porta Portese—just across the Tiber at the Sublicio Bridge *(Ponte Sublicio)*. Invariably jammed, Porta Portese operates from dawn to about 1 p.m. but *only on Sundays*. The flea market's

The annual Coronari antique fair attracts Romans and tourists alike.

cluttered stalls offer everything from refrigerators to kittens, with the emphasis on clothing.

Although prices may be marked and are often lower than in regular shops, by all means do haggle—everybody does.

Some real bargains can be found: you might buy two or three real silk ties for less than the normal shop price of one, for example. And the Abruzzi peasant bedspreads and rugs are among the market's very best buys. But there is an immense amount of suspect merchandise: shoddy plastics, "instant" antiques or artefacts, fabrics with machine flaws, hippy jewellery, pets with worms.

One entire section of the sprawling market is given over to car parts. They're astonishingly cheap because—it's universally assumed in Rome—they come from stolen cars which have been professionally stripped.

Adding to the fascinating atmosphere are wandering minstrels, fire-eaters and other showmen and pedlars from many other countries, including such unlikely places as Ethiopia and the Soviet Union.

You'll certainly see gypsies begging. You probably *won't* see pickpockets, but they'll inevitably be there.

Leave your passport and unneeded money behind when you visit **Porta Portese**. If you decide upon a major purchase, you can make arrangements to pick it up or have it delivered against payment later. Traveller's cheques are accepted at many of the market's stalls.

Even if you plan not to, you'll probably buy something. In any event, don't miss this entertaining market, a Roman version of an oriental bazaar.

During the week, Rome has two other outdoor markets far off the overtrodden tourist beat, where clothing and gift items are considerably cheaper than in regular shops. **Via Sannio**, which begins at Piazzale Appio by the Basilica of St. John Lateran, somewhat resembles a combination army-surplus store and Middle-Eastern market. Good but not fancy clothes, shoes, silverware from North Africa, carpets, handicrafts, coins and many leather or suede items are sold.

Piazza Vittorio Emanuele II (known as simply *Piazza* or *Mercato Vittorio*), four blocks from Termini railway station, features similar good-value clothing and Rome's best poultry and game stalls, along with novelty items, canaries and more exotic birds. Here, too, the wise shopper resorts to bargaining.

If it's not bargains but local

Could you face plucking one?

colour you are after, there is obviously nothing to beat the **flower market** in Via Trionfale, open on Tuesday mornings.

Each and every quarter has its own food market; for the bigger and better, try the Trionfale quarter, or the main fruit and vegetable market in Via Ostiense (open daily). Or what about the one at Campo de'Fiori where the people are as cheerful as the fruit—and the noise is deafening?

Quieter, and in another vein, Piazza Fontanella Borghese's Sunday market has exhibitions of engravings of Rome.

Bargaining

Roman shopkeepers will rarely be offended if you try to bargain; often they expect it, though the custom is slowly dying out. While bargaining in smart boutiques or city-centre luxury stores is probably a futile exercise, you may be given a discount *(sconto)* to "round off" the price of a major purchase—but not if you don't request it.

In smaller shops, friendly negotiating often cuts 10 per cent off the price, or the shop owner may throw in a free knicknack instead, particularly for female customers. The key to successful bargaining is to offer a price *far* lower than you expect to pay, and then to exhibit growing disinterest as the price rises toward your private maximum. On occasion a shopper may achieve a saving by agreeing to buy two of the items being bargained for.

Souvenirs

Airport and hotel souvenir stands are best avoided in Rome—prices are invariably higher than elsewhere. Similarly, tourist shops around St. Peter's charge more for religious mementos (which probably have not, despite sales claims, been "personally blessed by His Holiness") than do small Catholic speciality stores in sidestreets in the town centre across the river.

You'll find a plethora everywhere of cheap ceramic and plastic souvenirs of Rome, ashtrays, matchboxes, purses, pennants, and what not with embossed or painted landmarks. A better buy would be prints of old or modern Roman scenes. News-stands and bookshops also carry a large variety of excellent picture books of Rome; those with Italian texts cost less.

Wining and Dining

Doing as the Romans do so enthusiastically, visitors should plan to spend a good deal more time at meals than they normally do at home. Italians enjoy the conviviality that mealtimes offer, and a meal can easily become a major social occasion. Both lunch and dinner can linger on for hours, so the tourist who has been used to the eat-and-run or quick-lunch philosophy should slow down, take his time and enjoy the fine food Rome has to offer. The experience should be rewarding, perhaps too much so for some waistlines...

Just a fork, no spoon–it takes practice.

Restaurants and cafés

To rub shoulders with Rome's "smart set" costs money. At cafés and restaurants on the Piazza del Popolo and Piazza Navona, you pay for the chic as well as your *aperitivo,* and the prices of foreign alcoholic beverages are ruinous. Rome has countless other pleasant restaurants and outdoor cafés where ordinary people relax; that's a better way to "feel" the city and at a comforting saving.

A good rule of thumb is to avoid places with signs in English, German and French—they're geared to tourists, with prices therefore higher.

In theory, a *ristorante* is supposed to be a fancier and larger establishment than a family-style *trattoria.* But in Rome the distinction is blurred beyond recognition: they're both ways of saying restaurant, as is the less frequently used *osteria.*

In summer, it's an extremely pleasant custom to go a short way out of Rome to one of the many country inns for lunch or dinner. These sprawling and rustic places along such roads as Via Cassia and Via Flaminia are invariably cooler. They feature huge buffet-style tables of *antipasto* and all manner of grilled meats.

Roman restaurants usually serve from about 12.30 to 3 p.m. and from 7.30 p.m. to midnight, and each is closed one day a week. It's wise to book a table by telephone, particularly if you want to dine at peak hours (around 1.30 and 9.30 p.m.).

The strictly Italian snack bar or *tavola calda* ("hot table") offers usually palatable pasta and other snacks, sandwiches and salads, at a fraction of restaurant prices. They're crowded but quick; you may have to eat standing up. Pizza parlours, or *pizzerie,* are found throughout Rome. Snack bars are open from early morning until late at night, often till way past midnight, without interruption, as are ordinary bars and cafés which always have sandwiches and other snacks.

The cuisine

While the quality of the Roman cuisine falls short of the superb food characteristic of northern Italy, the city does offer—at generally much lower prices—a splendid variety of pasta dishes (the traditional first course),

Delicacies from Italy and abroad.

some very satisfying main dishes and excellent vegetables, fruit and wines.

If the pasta course alone is almost enough for you, it's perfectly acceptable (and often wise) to follow with nothing heavier than a salad, fruit or cheese, skipping the main dishes. Alternatively, one can always order a half-portion *(mezza porzione)* of pasta, or forego it entirely, opting instead perhaps for *antipasto* or another non-pasta starter.

Pasta. This is usually only the first of at least three courses for Italians. Rare is the Roman *trattoria* or *ristorante* which doesn't serve at least one outstanding speciality. Pasta itself comes in myriad forms. Macaroni, ravioli and spaghetti are familiar abroad, but for the Italian housewife and her pasta-loving family, the choice is enormous. Here's a list which you can try to work your way through: *spaghetti, fettuccine, tagliatelle, pappardelle, rigatoni, penne, linguini, bucatini, ravioli, agnolotti, tortellini, tortelloni, tonnarelli, cannelloni* and *lasagne.* (Remember, there's still dessert when you have finished!) 85

But what counts is the sauce, and that's where Roman cooks often excel:

Amatriciana: tomato, bacon, onion, red peppers, garlic

Arrabbiata: tomato, garlic, hot red peppers, parsley

Bolognese (or *Ragù*): minced meat, tomato, herbs

Boscaiola: tunny (tuna), tomato, garlic, parsley

Caccia (or *Lepre*): game (rabbit, etc.), cream or tomato

Carbonara: beaten egg, diced bacon, cheese, butter or oil, basil

Checco: tomato and fresh basil

Ciociara: peas, diced ham, mushrooms

Crema: cream, Parmesan cheese, butter

Marinara: tomato, garlic, olives, hot red peppers, capers, parsley

Olio-aglio-peperoncino: oil, garlic, hot red peppers, parsley

Pescatore: seafood, tomato or white wine, parsley

Pesto (genovese): basil, oil, pine nuts, cheese, garlic

Pomodoro: tomato, garlic, parsley

Many Roman restaurants are proud of their house pasta, which may be named after the cook, his mother or his birthplace. Be sure to ask for a description of the speciality.

Cafés are a way of life.

Main course. This, second course, will usually be meat, game or fish.

The tastiest beef, offered by better Roman restaurants, is Florentine T-bone steak *(bistecca alla fiorentina),* usually charcoal-grilled. It's expensive by local standards, but the quality compares favourably with the finest steaks abroad. A *filetto* (fillet) or *bistecca* (regular steak) will cost less.

A number of Roman or displaced Tuscan cooks specialize in game *(caccia)* and fowl *(pollame).* In season, try boar *(cinghiale)* in a sweet-and-sour sauce *(agrodolce).*

The seafood saga in Rome is rather sad. Because the nearby Tyrrhenian Sea is steadily becoming fished out, not to mention polluted, very little fresh fish is available in the capital. Waiters will only sometimes admit, when asked, that the attractive fish selection they're offering is frozen. Frozen or not, seafood is never cheap in Roman restaurants; often it's twice the price of meat!

Vegetables—often eaten as a cold or hot separate course with butter, or olive oil and lemon *(all'agro)*—are a year-round delight in Rome. Spinach *(spinaci)*, endives [US chicory] *(cicoria)*, courgettes *(zucchine)* and eggplant or aubergine *(melanzana)* are particularly popular. And many restaurants offer butter beans *(fagioli)*, either in a thick soup or as a side dish with a strong hint of garlic *(aglio)*.

Cheese. Persevering stoutly, you'll find still more delights when the cheeseboard is placed before you. Italy's most famous cheeses, the mild *Bel Paese* and the piquant, blue *Gorgonzola,* are always there. But also look for the creamy and tangy *Taleggio,* the flavourful *Casciotto* from Tuscany or *Provolone,* a firm cheese available either in a sharp or a mild version. *Mozzarella,* the chewy, all-purpose cheese which used to be made from

Gelateria = *ice-cream shop.*

buffalo's milk, is eaten alone, deep-fried *(mozzarella in carrozza),* or in a salad with tomatoes and fresh basil *(basilico).*

Dessert. For dessert, you're likely to be overwhelmed by the sight of a tray loaded with gooey pastry, including *zuppa inglese,* the famous Italian—not English—dessert made with liquored sponge-cake and creamy custard, slightly reminiscent of English trifle. Even Romans may balk at that, in which case they'd probably choose fresh fruit *(frutta fresca)* or ice-cream *(gelato),* justly and universally admired for its rich, creamy texture and full flavour. In winter, blood oranges *(aranci Tarocchi)* are a special treat.

87

Beverages

Coffee. After all that, it's no wonder that an espresso, or a double espresso *(un doppio),* is considered absolutely essential. Coffee is very good almost everywhere in Rome. In summer you may opt for a *granita di caffè,* coffee over crushed ice.

At this stage, the restaurateur will sometimes offer, free of charge, an after-dinner liqueur, appealingly called a *digestivo.* After-dinner liqueurs may be bitter or thickly sweet; all are very potent.

Wine. During the one-and-a-half to two hours it normally takes to finish off a Roman meal, consumption of wine is, of course, *de rigueur.* Most restaurants are proud of their open, house wine, served in one-quarter, one-half or one-litre carafes (about a quart). The white, usually from the Alban Hills south of Rome, is generally known as Frascati or Castelli Romani. It's light, dry and pleasant. For a slightly higher charge you might prefer a bottle of Tuscan or Umbrian white. Sicilian and Sardinian whites, less often available in Rome, are perhaps even better choices.

The open red wine in Roman restaurants is acceptable but not overly exciting. However, bottled Tuscan Chiantis are omnipresent, and such north-Italian standbys as Barolo, Gattinara and Valpolicella are worth asking for. Better restaurants will always have a wine list, and even the tiniest *trattoria* will offer a decent selection of bottled vintages. Specialists look for *Riserva* on the label.

Beer. This is also always available and growing in popularity. Italian brands are less strong than northern European beers.

Water. Still imitating the Romans, you'll want to order a bottle (half-litre or litre) of mineral water *(acqua minerale)* as well with your meal (see WATER, page 123). Gourmets absolutely insist it helps digestion, and wine novices may want to dilute their red or white wine with some of the usually carbonated bottled water.

Breakfast

The traditional Roman breakfast consists of a cup of *cappuccino* (coffee with whipped milk, dusted with cocoa) and pastry. In season, fresh orange or lemon juice *(spremuta di arancia* or *limone*) is widely available. Many hotels now also serve a more substantial breakfast in the English or American style.

Prices and tips
While some small restaurants offer a fixed-price, three-course meal (*menù turistico* or *prezzo fisso*) which will save money, you'll almost always get better food by ordering dishes individually.

Warning: all restaurants must now issue a formal receipt indicating the sales tax or VAT *(I.V.A.)*. A customer may be stopped outside the premises and fined if unable to produce a receipt. The bill usually includes cover *(coperto)* and service *(servizio)* charges as well.

It's customary to leave the waiter about 10 per cent of the bill—the Romans do, because it's expected but also because restaurant service is generally attentively excellent. When a wine waiter counsels and serves you, a tip to him of several hundred lire is appropriate. Never tip the owner, no matter how much he may fuss over you—he'd be offended.

Open-air art and dining belong together.

TO HELP YOU ORDER...

Good evening. I'd like a table for three.	Buona sera. Vorrei un tavolo per tre persone.
Could we have a table outside?	Potremmo avere un tavolo all'esterno ?
Do you have a set menu?	Avete un menù a prezzo fisso ?
I'd like a/an/some...	Vorrei...

ashtray	**un portacenere**	mineral water	**dell'acqua minerale**
beer	**una birra**		
bread	**del pane**	napkin	**un tovagliolo**
butter	**del burro**	olive oil	**dell'olio d'oliva**
chair	**una sedia**	pepper	**del pepe**
coffee	**un caffè**	potatoes	**delle patate**
condiments	**del condimento**	salad	**dell'insalata**
cream	**della panna**	salt	**del sale**
cutlery	**delle posate**	sandwich	**un sandwich**
dessert	**un dessert**	serviette	**un tovagliolo**
fish	**del pesce**	soup	**una minestra**
fork	**una forchetta**	spoon	**un cucchiaio**
fruit	**della frutta**	sugar	**dello zucchero**
glass	**un bicchiere**	tea	**un tè**
ice-cream	**un gelato**	toothpick	**uno stuzzica-denti**
knife	**un coltello**		
meat	**della carne**	(iced) water	**dell'acqua (fredda)**
menu	**un menù**		
milk	**del latte**	wine	**del vino**

...AND READ THE MENU

aglio	garlic	**antipasto**	starter (appetizer)
agnello	lamb		
albicocche	apricots	**arancia**	orange
al forno	baked	**arrosto**	roast
anguilla	eel	**baccalà**	dried cod
anguria	watermelon	**braciola**	chop
anitra	duck	**calamari**	squid

carciofi alla romana	artichokes with garlic and wine
cervello fritto	deep-fried brains
cicoria	endive (Am. chicory)
ciliege	cherries
cinghiale	wild boar
cipolle	onions
coniglio	rabbit
cozze	mussels
crepes al formaggio	cheese crêpes
crostacei	shellfish
dentice	dentex
fagiano	pheasant
fagioli	beans
faraona	guinea fowl
fegato alla veneziana	liver and onions
fichi	figs
formaggio	cheese
fragole	strawberries
fritto	fried
frutti di mare	seafood
funghi	mushrooms
gamberi	scampi, prawns
gnocchi	dumplings
insalata	salad
lamponi	raspberries
lombata di maiale	pork tenderloin
mandorle	almonds
mela	apple
melanzana	aubergine (eggplant)
merluzzo	cod
minestra	soup
olive	olives
peperoni	peppers, pimentos
pera	pear
pesca	peach
pesce	fish
pesce spada	swordfish
piccata al limone	veal scallops in lemon sauce
polenta	purée of maize (cornmeal)
pollo	chicken
pomodoro	tomato
porchetta	baby pork done on a spit
prosciutto (e melone o fichi)	ham (with melon or figs)
prugna	plum
quaglia	quail
riso	rice
rognoni	kidneys
salsa	sauce
saltimbocca	veal scallops topped with sage and ham
seppia	cuttlefish
sogliola	sole
spigola	sea bass
spinaci	spinach
stufato	stew
tartufi	truffles
triglia	red mullet
trippe	tripe
uova	eggs
uva	grapes
vitello	veal
vitello tonnato	cold veal in a sauce of tuna, mayonnaise, capers
vongole	clams
zuppa	soup

Relaxing in Rome

Because of the heat in Rome during much of the year, by all means adopt the local wisdom of relaxing whenever possible. Between sightseeing or shopping jaunts during the day, a drink, an espresso or a dish of ice-cream at an outdoor café is both prudent and pleasant. People-watching is almost as good, and certainly cheaper, from a bench in any of Rome's beautiful parks or gardens. If you're young at heart, you'll find swarms of company lounging on the Spanish Steps, in Piazza Navona or Piazza Santa Maria in Trastevere, and along the shaded banks of the Tiber.

Night-life. Only the scantest traces remain of Rome's fabled *dolce vita*. A few starlets and aging aristocratic playboys may still be seen at the cripplingly expensive cafés on the Via Veneto, and a minor-league jetset frequents Piazza del Popolo and a handful of semi-private, late-night discotheques, but most of the effervescence has long since gone out of after-dark Roman social life. On the rare occasions when a genuine celebrity is out on the town, you'll know by the popping flashbulbs of Rome's roving freelance photographers, the *papparazzi*.

In a capital with remarkably little night-life, the most popular custom is to linger well past midnight over dinner at the innumerable outdoor restaurants where minstrels and guitarists hold noisily forth (see WINING AND DINING, page 83). Romans rarely enter the overpriced bars and cocktail lounges in the hotel district around Via Veneto.

The city has perhaps a dozen discotheques similar to those elsewhere in Europe. Familiarly, they're deafening, dark, smoky and very crowded. Not all charge entrance fees, but drinks are never cheap. A few larger establishments have dance floors and cabarets; and there's dancing in the lounges of some hotels. From time to time, jazz, folk, vocal or pop concerts are held in theatres, though Rome rarely attracts topflight international entertainers.

Tourists seeking companionship will have little difficulty finding it. For men, a greater challenge may well be shaking off the relentless street-corner playmates. If you're not in-

There's always activity at the foot of the Spanish Steps.

terested, keep walking and keep quiet, and the Roman maidens will seek another target.

Music. Almost every summer evening, there's outdoor opera in the spectacular setting of the ruined Baths of Caracalla *(Terme di Caracalla),* an easy bus or taxi ride from the centre of town. Your hotel desk-clerk can arrange tickets for this tourist favourite (and for the equally popular sound and light performances at the Forum and outside Rome in Tivoli). The much admired St. Cecilia Conservatory Orchestra and occasional visiting groups give classical music concerts throughout the year, sometimes under the stars at the Basilica of Maxentius *(Massenzio)* alongside the Forum.

Cinema. Rome has nearly 200 cinemas, but never more than three which show films in their original language. Sub-titles are not used: foreign films are dubbed in Italian. Rome's *Daily News* mentions whatever English-language film is playing at the city's one small cinema (the *Pasquino* in Trastevere), devoted solely to British and American productions, and will also report the rare presentation of a foreign film in the original at a Rome cinema.

At times, small "film studios" may show a week or two of non-Italian films, particularly classics. Rome's cinemas are expensive and almost always filled to capacity, even for the 93

Italians are cinema lovers.

late-night showing at 10.30 or 11 p.m. But an Italian film is a good way to improve your understanding of the language and mingle with the Romans. Italian cinema commercials which precede feature films are often hilarious.

Theatre. Rome's theatre is generally considered undistinguished and, again, performances are almost always in Italian, though English plays are occasionally staged. A better bet for the family might be a circus—there's usually one somewhere in Rome.

SPORTS

Sports facilities are limited in Rome, and those which do exist are often private.

Swimming. Rome is only some 19 miles from the beaches of the Tyrrhenian Sea but, sadly, swimming there can no longer be recommended in view of the serious pollution. If swim you must, Rome has a variety of pools *(piscina)*. The municipal pools tend to be very crowded but are clean, have good lifeguards and offer adequate facilities. Some luxury hotels permit non-residents to use their pools for an admission fee, usually rather high.

Tennis. Tennis courts, usually of clay, abound in Rome, but most belong to private clubs. Your hotel porter may be able to make an arrangement for you. Some de-luxe hotels have their own courts available to outsiders, but they are usually expensive. It's best to book a court in advance. Rackets are very rarely on hire.

Horse-riding. Ask your desk-clerk to call any of the half-dozen riding stables in and around Rome. Fees are hourly and relatively cheap, and instructors are available.

If you'd rather watch and wager, flat-racing, trotting and greyhound meetings are held most weeks at courses near Rome.

How to Get There

If the choice of ways to go is bewildering, the complexity of fares and regulations can be downright stupefying. A reliable travel agent will have full details of all the latest flight possibilities, fares and regulations.

BY AIR

Scheduled Flights

Rome's Fiumicino airport (officially known as Leonardo da Vinci airport) is on many important intercontinental air routes, and is also linked by frequent direct services to numerous cities in Europe, Middle East and Africa.

Charter Flights and Package Tours

From the British Isles: if you decide on a package tour, read your contract carefully before you sign. Most tour agents recommend cancellation insurance, a modestly priced safeguard; you lose no money if illness or accident forces you to cancel your holiday.

From North America: ABC (advance booking charter) flights cost less than APEX fares, but go to fewer cities. Tickets must be bought 30 days in advance, and flights are open to all.

BY CAR

By car ferry: if you decide to take your car across the Channel and then drive to Rome, make sure of your passage by booking well in advance. The principal car ferry routes are:

Via France: Dover–Boulogne/Calais/Dunkirk; Newhaven–Dieppe; Southampton–Cherbourg/Le Havre; Folkestone–Boulogne/Calais; Ramsgate–Dunkirk.

Via Belgium: Dover–Ostend/Zeebrugge; Folkestone–Ostend/Zeebrugge; Hull–Zeebrugge.

Via Holland: Harwich–Hook van Holland; Hull–Rotterdam, Sheerness–Vlissingen.

By hovercraft: in 35 to 45 minutes for approximately the same price as the ferry, you can cross from Dover to Calais or Boulogne.

By rail: cars can be carried on special wagons with the driver travelling on the same train. Starting points include Ostend, Boulogne, Paris and Cologne. These express car-sleeper trains leave in the evening and arrive the next morning in Milan, where you can continue on to Rome by train or car.

BY RAIL

In Great Britain and Ireland, British Rail and its agents issue tickets to Rome with a validity of two months. Stops are allowed at intermediate points en route.

Eurailpass: Anyone except residents of Europe can travel on a flat-rate, unlimited mileage ticket valid for first-class rail travel anywhere in western Europe outside of Great Britain. The Eurailpass may be purchased for periods of 2 or 3 weeks, 1, 2 or 3 months. Eurail Youthpass offers 2 months of second-class travel to anyone under 26. These tickets also offer discounts on other forms of transportation. You must buy your pass before leaving home.

Inter-Rail Card: This ticket permits 30 days of unlimited rail travel in participating European countries to people under 26. In the country of issue, fares are given a 50% discount.

Italian Tourist Ticket: Unlimited first- or second-class travel on the entire national rail network for 8, 15, 21 or 30 days. May be bought in your home country or in Italy.

Kilometric Ticket: The most interesting feature of this pass is that it may be used by up to 5 people, even if not related. Good for 20 trips or 3,000 kilometres (1,875 miles), first or second class. Can be purchased at home or in Italy.

BY COACH

Express buses run between London and Rome all year round. For details, contact a reliable travel agent.

When to Go

In climate as in politics, Rome can be a city of extremes. From mid-June to mid-September, temperatures range from hot to very hot. During the winter you can expect it to be cool and at times rainy or even icily cold with perhaps a bit of snow. However, it's a rare winter week without at least one day of warm sunshine. The weather is generally very pleasant in the spring and autumn.

If you're particularly interested in Rome's artistic and cultural treasures, it's best to go off season or in early or late summer when the city is less crowded and the air agreeably warm.

	J	F	M	A	M	J	J	A	S	O	N	D
Air temperature												
Max. F°	62	57	71	79	86	86	94	93	86	82	68	62
C°	17	14	22	26	30	30	35	34	30	28	20	17
Min. F°	32	37	28	44	46	55	57	61	55	41	39	32
C°	0	3	-2	7	8	13	14	16	13	5	4	0
Days of sunshine	7	17	10	10	10	14	26	24	24	23	14	11

Planning Your Budget

To give you an idea of what to expect, here's a list of average prices in lire (L.). However, remember that all prices must be regarded as *approximate,* and that the inflation rate is high.

Airport transfer. Bus from Fiumicino or Ciampino airports to Termini railway station L. 4,000, taxi from Fiumicino or Ciampino to city centre L. 40,000–45,000.

Baby-sitters. L. 10,000–15,000 per hour, plus transport.

Buses (city) **and metro.** Standard fare L. 400.

Camping (high season). Adults L. 5,000 per person per night, children L. 4,000, caravan (trailer) or camper L. 8,000, tent/car L. 5,500, motorbike L. 2,500.

Care hire (international company). *Fiat Panda 45* L. 35,300 per day, L. 554 per km., L. 569,000 per week with unlimited mileage. *Alfa 33* L. 62,300 per day, L. 750 per km., L. 903,000 per week with unlimited mileage. Add 18% tax.

Cigarettes (packet of 20). Italian brands L. 1,000–1,800, imported brands L. 2,000–2,500.

Entertainment. Cinema L. 3,000–6,000, discotheque (entry and one drink) L. 15,000–30,000.

Hairdressers. *Woman's* shampoo and set or blow-dry L. 15,000–25,000, permanent wave L. 35,000–70,000. *Man's* haircut L. 12,000–15,000.

Hotels (double room with bath, summer season). ***** L. 250,000–400,000, **** L. 100,000–250,000, *** L. 90,000–125,000, ** L. 60,000–90,000, * L. 50,000–75,000.

Meals and drinks. Continental breakfast L. 5,000–15,000, lunch/dinner in fairly good establishment L. 30,000–70,000, coffee served at a table L. 2,000–4,000, served at the bar L. 400–500, bottle of wine L. 4,000 and up, soft drinks L. 2,000 and up, aperitif L. 2,500 and up.

Museums. L. 1,000–4,000 (state museums are free on the first and third Saturday of the month and the second and fourth Sunday; municipal museums are free on Sundays).

Taxis. L. 1,200 for first 300 metres, L. 90 for each additional 250 metres, L. 700 surcharge at end of journey whatever the charge on meter. Sundays and holidays L. 900 extra, night charge (10 p.m.–7 a.m.) L. 1,500. Some taxis have their meters adjusted to a starting rate of L. 2,000 with L. 90 per 250 metres.

BLUEPRINT for a Perfect Trip

An A-Z Summary of Practical Information and Facts

Contents

A star (*) following an entry indicates that relevant prices are to be found on page 98.

Listed after some entries is the appropriate Italian translation, usually in the singular, plus a number of phrases that may come in handy during your stay in Italy.

A **ACCOMMODATION*** (see also CAMPING). Rome's array of lodgings (some 1,300 hotels) ranges from small, family-style boarding-houses *(pensione)* to de-luxe hotels *(albergo* or *hotel)*. During the summer, booking ahead is very important, but for the rest of the year you can normally find accommodation in your preferred category without difficulty. The Italian Tourist Office has up-to-date hotel information at the air terminal at Termini railway station. If you have trouble sleeping, be sure to ask for a quiet room *(una stanza tranquilla)*—this will face onto an enclosed courtyard, air shaft or, if you're lucky, a garden.

If you're planning to walk to most of Rome's sights, as you should, book at a hotel in the *centro storico* (historical centre), rather than in the residential areas or suburbs. The saving in transport costs should compensate for the slightly higher hotel or boarding-house rates in the centre of town. In the high tourist season (July and August), many hotels try to insist that you take breakfast with them. If possible avoid this, as hotel breakfasts are invariably more expensive (and less interesting) than having a *cappuccino* and pastry at a stand-up bar—as the Romans do.

As much as 20% in taxes and service charges may be added to the hotel rates listed on page 98. Off-season rates are lower, but not much. A few major hotels have swimming pools and tennis courts.

On its periphery, Rome has several motels. Some Roman Catholic orders take in guests at very reasonable rates.

Youth hostels *(ostello della gioventù)* are open to holders of membership cards issued by the International Youth Hostels Association, or by the A.I.G. *(Associazione Italiana Alberghi per la Gioventù)*, the Italian Youth Hostels Association, at:

Lungotevere Maresciallo Cadorna, 61; tel. 3960009

Day hotels (see also p. 19). Rome has about five *alberghi diurni*— "day-time hotels"—one of them situated at Termini railway station. These have no sleeping accommodation but provide bathrooms, toilet facilities, hairdressers, etc. Most close at midnight.

I'd like a single/double room.	**Vorrei una camera singola/ matrimoniale.**
with bath/shower	**con bagno/doccia**
What's the rate per night?	**Qual è il prezzo per una notte?**

AIRPORTS *(aeroporto)*. Rome is served by two airports, Leonardo da Vinci, commonly referred to as Fiumicino (at the seaside, 30 km. south-west of the city), and Ciampino (16 km. south-east by the Via Appia Nuova). Fiumicino mainly handles scheduled air traffic, while Ciampino is used by most charter companies. Note that Fiumicino has two terminals, one for domestic and one for international flights. They are a five-minute walk apart.

It has become conventional tourist wisdom to travel light, and that is particularly good advice when visiting Rome; air travellers sometimes find they must carry their own bags because ground staff are on strike.

Airport information:

Fiumicino, tel. 6 01 21
Ciampino, tel. 46 94

Ground transport*. Both airports are linked to the city air terminal (at Termini railway station) in the centre of Rome by frequent services of inexpensive public buses.

City air terminal: Via Giolitti, 36; tel. 46 46 13

In normal traffic, allow an hour to get to Fiumicino by taxi, 45 minutes to Ciampino. Unlicensed taxis, *taxi pirati*, may charge more than twice the rates listed on page 98.

Check-in time is 1 hour before departure for international flights, 25 minutes before domestic flights. Luggage may be checked in only at the airport. A few hours before leaving Rome, have your hotel receptionist telephone both the airport and the city air terminal to inquire about any delay or sudden bus strike.

Domestic air travel. There are good services from Rome to Milan, Genoa, Turin, Naples, Cagliari, Palermo, Bari and Venice, and less frequent flights to other Italian cities.

A Rome has a third airport, Urbe, in Via Salaria, 225 (north-east of the city centre), reserved for private planes, where light aircraft can be hired. Phone 8 12 05 71.

Porter!	**Facchino!**
Take these bags to the bus/taxi, please.	**Mi porti queste valige fino all'autobus/al taxi, per favore.**

B **BABY-SITTERS*.** Hotel receptionists can usually arrange for a reliable baby-sitter. If you don't stay in a hotel, consult the *Rome Daily American* or the *International Daily News* or one of the Italian-language newspapers which always carry baby-sitter advertisements (in English or under the heading "Bambinaia"). A number of agencies are also listed in English in the telephone directory under "Baby Sitter" and "Baby Parking".

Can you get me a baby-sitter for tonight?	**Può trovarmi una bambinaia per questa sera?**

C **CAMPING*.** Rome and the surrounding countryside have some 25 official campsites, most of them equipped with electricity, water and toilet facilities. They are listed in the yellow pages of the telephone directory under "Campeggio". You can also contact the Ente Provinciale per il Turismo (see TOURIST INFORMATION OFFICES) for a comprehensive list of sites, rates and complete details. The Touring Club Italiano and the Automobile Club d'Italia publish lists of campsites and tourist villages, which can be bought in bookstores or referred to in E. P. T. offices.

In Italy, you may camp freely outside of sites if you obtain permission either from the owner of the property or from the local authorities; in the metropolitan Rome area, this is, of course, not recommended. For your personal safety you should choose sites where there are other campers.

If you enter Italy with a caravan (trailer) you must be able to show an inventory (with two copies) of the material and equipment in the caravan: dishes, linen, etc.

May we camp here?	**Possiamo campeggiare qui?**
Is there a campsite near here?	**C'è un campeggio qui vicino?**
We have a tent/caravan (trailer).	**Abbiamo la tenda/la roulotte.**

CAR HIRE* *(autonoleggio).* The major international car rental firms have offices in the main cities and at the airports; they are listed in the yellow pages of the telephone directory. The hotel receptionist may be able to recommend a less expensive local firm. You need a valid driving licence. Minimum age varies from 21 to 25 according to the company. A deposit is often required except for credit card holders. Most agencies offer a range of Fiats; larger Italian and foreign models are less frequently available. It is possible to rent a car in one Italian city and turn it in at another. Ask for any available seasonal deals.

I'd like to rent a car (tomorrow).	**Vorrei noleggiare un'automobile (per domani).**
for one day	**per un giorno**
for a week	**per una settimana**

CIGARETTES, CIGARS, TOBACCO* *(sigarette, sigari, tabacco).* Sold under state monopoly, tobacco products in Italy are price-controlled. Dark and light tobaccos are available, as are most well-known cigars and pipe tobacco. The cheapest Italian cigarettes are considered somewhat rough by most foreigners. Local and imported brands are on sale in tobacco shops *(tabaccaio)* bearing a large white "T" on a dark background, not at kiosks, although hotel news-stands may have some cigarettes. "T" shops also sell postcards and stamps.

I'd like a packet of ...	**Vorrei un pacchetto di ...**
with/without filter	**con/senza filtro**
I'd like a box of matches.	**Per favore, mi dia una scatola di fiammiferi.**

CLOTHING. From May to September you should take along cotton summer clothes with a jacket or shawl for the evening. Comfortable walking shoes are indispensable. Since in the normal course of events hardly a drop of rain falls in Rome in summer, there's no reason to bring a raincoat and certainly not an overcoat. This is an informal city (though even the casually dressed Romans dress smartly) and few restaurants insist on a tie. And since eating is outdoors for much of the year, even a jacket is unnecessary. However, in winter or for better restaurants or parties, dark suits or cocktail dresses are recommended.

Slacks for women are acceptable everywhere with the possible exception of a few churches. But shorts and bare-backed dresses are strictly forbidden in such churches as St. Peter's, and you may have to cover your bare arms.

At Rome's swimming pools or while sunbathing at nearby beaches (sea-swimming not advisable—see page 94), Italian women wear very brief bikinis, and men's trunks are often not notably larger.

COMMUNICATIONS

Post offices *(ufficio postale)* handle telegrams, mail and money transfers, and some have public telephones. Stamps are also sold at tobacconists *(tabaccaio)* and at some hotel desks. Postboxes are red; the slot marked *Per la città* is for Rome mail only, *Altre destinazioni* for post going to any other destination.

At times a national disaster of storied proportions, Italy's postal service normally functions decently, though as a general rule your postcards home will arrive long after you do. The Vatican's post office functions very well for outgoing mail. You must buy Vatican City stamps and post your letters on the premises.

Post office **hours** are normally from 8.15 a.m. to 2 p.m., Monday to Friday, Saturday till 12 noon or 1 p.m.

Rome's main post office in Piazza San Silvestro is open from 8.30 a.m. to 9 p.m., Saturday from 8 a.m. to 12 noon.

Poste restante (general delivery). Unless it's absolutely essential, don't arrange to receive mail during a brief visit to Rome: have people cable or telephone your hotel, it's more reliable. You can nevertheless have your mail addressed c/o *Fermo Posta* (poste restante or general delivery) to Rome's central post office:

Mr. John Smith
Fermo Posta
Piazza San Silvestro
Posta Centrale di Roma, Italy.

Take your passport along as identification when you go to pick up mail from the post office; a small charge is made.

Telegrams. The main post office (see above) is open 24 hours a day for this service. Night letters or night-rate telegrams are delivered the following morning and are much cheaper than straight-rate telegrams.

Telephone *(telefono).* Glass-enclosed booths are scattered throughout the city, and almost every bar and café has a public telephone, indicated by a yellow sign showing a telephone dial outside. Older types of public payphones require tokens *(gettoni;* available from machines [generally installed next to the telephone] and at bars, hotels, post offices and tobacconists'), modern ones, with two separate slots, take both *gettoni* and 100- and 200-lira coins.

If the phone is labelled "Teleselezione", you can make direct international calls, but be sure to have a great many coins or tokens (the cashier in the café will buy back unused *gettoni*).

International telephone offices are located next to the main post office in Piazza San Silvestro, at the airports and railway station, and in some local post offices.

For a reverse-charge (collect) call, specify *chiamata R* (pronounced *kyah-maa-tah ay-ray*).

A few useful numbers:

Local directory and other Italian inquiries	12
Operator for Europe	15
Operator for intercontinental calls	170
Telegrams	186

Give me ... *gettoni,* please.	**Per favore, mi dia ... gettoni.**
Can you get me this number in ...?	**Può passarmi questo numero a ...?**
Have you received any mail for ...?	**C'è posta per ...?**
I'd like a stamp for this letter/postcard.	**Desidero un francobollo per questa lettera/cartolina.**
express (special delivery)	**espresso**
airmail	**via aerea**
registered	**raccomandata**
I want to send a telegram to ...	**Desidero mandare un telegramma a ...**

COMPLAINTS. Complaining about inadequate facilities or services in Italy is one of the easier ways of wasting your valuable holiday time. Any remarks of this sort will release such a flood of agitated Italian with gestures that you'll wish you hadn't bothered!

To avoid unpleasant situations, observe the cardinal rule of commerce in Italy: come to an agreement in advance—the price, the supplements, the taxes and the services to be received, preferably in writing. If that fails, try appealing to the local tourist office or to the police. The threat of a formal declaration to the police should be effective in such cases as overcharging for car repairs, but this will consume hours or even days of your visit. A threat of recourse to your embassy or consulate will impress few, although this should certainly

C be your course of action in the event of any serious trouble with the police (as in a major car accident). Any complaint about a taxi fare should be settled by referring to a notice, in four languages, affixed by law in each taxi, specifying extra charges (airport runs, Sunday or holiday rates, night surcharge) in excess of the meter rate.

CONSULATES and EMBASSIES *(consolato; ambasciata).* Practically all countries of the world have embassies in Rome. If your embassy is not listed in the following, consult the telephone directory for its address:

Australia. Via Alessandria, 215; tel. 84 12 41

Canada. Via G. Battista De Rossi, 27; tel. 85 53 42

Eire. Via del Pozzetto, 105; tel. 6 78 25 41

South Africa. Piazza Monte Grappa, 4; tel. 3 60 84 41

United Kingdom. Via XX Settembre, 80; tel. 4 75 54 41

U.S.A. Via Vittorio Veneto, 119; tel. 46 74

Most consulates are open from Monday to Friday from about 9 a.m. to 5 p.m.—though some may close at lunch time. Many nations maintain separate embassies in Rome accredited to the Holy See.

CONVERTER CHARTS. For fluid and distance measures, see page 111. Italy uses the metric system.

Temperature

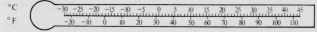

Length

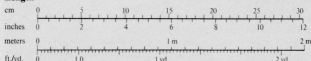

Weight

grams | 0 | 100 | 200 | 300 | 400 | 500 | 600 | 700 | 800 | 900 | 1 kg
ounces | 0 | 4 | 8 | 12 | 1 lb | 20 | 24 | 28 | 2 lb.

COURTESIES. See also MEETING PEOPLE. Less formal than many other Europeans, Italians nonetheless practise certain social courtesies. On entering and leaving a shop, restaurant or office, the expected greeting is always *buon giorno* (good morning) or *buona sera* (good evening). When approaching anyone with an inquiry, the correct form is *per favore* (please), and for any service say *grazie* (thanks), to which the reply is *prego* (don't mention it; you're welcome).

Introductions are usually accompanied by handshaking and the phrase *piacere* (it's a pleasure). With people you know well, *ciao* is the casual form of greeting or farewell.

The best way to address a waiter or waitress is by saying *senta* which means literally "listen" and is used to attract their attention. When wished *buon appetito* before starting a meal, reply *grazie, altrettanto* (the same to you).

How are you?	**Come sta?**
Very well, thanks.	**Molto bene, grazie.**

CRIME and THEFT. Petty theft is an endless annoyance, and it's better to be forewarned. Leave your documents and unneeded cash at your hotel, and keep what you do need in an inside pocket. Pickpockets and bag snatchers tend to frequent tourist areas. A popular technique is for one or two young thieves to cruise along on a motorscooter, slice the shoulder strap of a woman's bag and roar off with it.

As in many large cities, conmen, hawkers of stolen goods, prostitutes and pedlars of other illicit pleasures hang out near the major hotels. The best way to deal with them is simply to ignore them, even when they appear sincere and are well-dressed.

Thefts of cars or of their contents can best be avoided by emptying them of everything—not only of valuables. Leave the glove compartments empty and open to discourage prospective thieves. If your hotel has a private garage, leave your car there.

The political and social climate may be troubled, but violent crime concerning tourists is rare.

I want to report a theft.	**Voglio denunciare un furto.**
My wallet/handbag/passport/ ticket has been stolen.	**Mi hanno rubato il portafoglio/la borsa/il passaporto/il biglietto.**

CUSTOMS (*dogana*) **and ENTRY REGULATIONS.** For a stay of up to three months, a valid passport is sufficient for citizens of Australia,

Canada, New Zealand and U.S.A. Visitors from Eire and the United Kingdom need only an identity card to enter Italy.

Italian customs officials are unlikely to quibble over smaller points; they are interested mainly in detecting smuggled art treasures, currency or narcotics. If you're exporting archaeological relics, works of art, or gems, you should obtain a bill of sale and a permit from the government (this is normally handled by the dealer).

Here are some main items you can take into Italy and, when returning home, into your own country:

Entering Italy from:	Cigarettes		Cigars		Tobacco	Spirits		Wine
1)	200	or	50	or	250 g.	¾ l.	or	2 l.
2)	300	or	75	or	400 g.	1.5 l.	or	5 l.
3)	400	or	100	or	500 g.	¾ l.	or	2 l.
Into:								
Australia	200	or	250	or	250 g.	1 l.	or	1 l.
Canada	200	and	50	and	900 g.	1.1 l.	or	1.1 l.
Eire	200	or	50	or	250 g.	1 l.	and	2 l.
N. Zealand	200	or	50	or	250 g.	1.1 l.	and	4.5 l.
S. Africa	400	and	50	and	250 g.	1 l.	and	2 l.
U.K.	200	or	50	or	250 g.	1 l.	and	2 l.
U.S.A.	200	and	100	and	4)	1 l.	or	1 l.

1) within Europe from non-EEC countries
2) within Europe from EEC countries
3) countries outside Europe
4) a reasonable quantity

Currency restrictions. Non-residents may import or export up to L. 400,000 in local currency. In foreign currencies, tourists may import unlimited amounts, but to take the equivalent of more than L. 1,000,000 in or out of the country, you must fill out a V2 declaration form at the border upon entry.

I've nothing to declare.	**Non ho nulla da dichiarare.**
It's for my personal use.	**È per mio uso personale.**

DRIVING IN ITALY

Entering Italy. To bring your car into Italy you will need:

- an international driving licence (non-Europeans)
- car registration papers
- Green Card (an extension to your regular insurance policy, making it valid for foreign countries). Though not obligatory for EEC countries, it's still preferable to have it.
- national identity sticker for your car and the red warning triangle in case of breakdown.

Note: Before leaving home, check with your automobile association about the latest regulations concerning *petrol coupons* (that give tourists access to cheaper fuel) in Italy, as they are constantly changing.

Driving conditions. Drive on the right. Pass on the left. Traffic on major roads has the right of way over traffic entering from side roads, but this, like all other traffic regulations, is frequently ignored, so beware. At intersections of roads of similar importance, the car on the right theoretically has the right of way. When passing other vehicles, or remaining in the left-hand (passing) lane, keep your directional indicator flashing. On the *autostrada* (motorway or expressway) there's often a lane to the extreme right for very slow traffic. The motorways and most major national highways are of excellent quality, skilfully designed for fast driving. Each section of an *autostrada* requires the payment of a toll: you collect a card from an automatic machine and pay at the other end for the distance travelled. Try to stock up on 100-lira coins, since the toll booth attendants don't like making change.

On country roads and even many main highways, you'll encounter bicycles, motorscooters, three-wheeled vehicles, horse-drawn carts and even donkey caravans. Very often, such slow-moving vehicles have *no* lights, an obvious danger from dusk to dawn.

Last but not least: cars, buses, lorries (trucks) make use, indiscriminately, of their horns—in fact, blowing one's horn is an Italian pastime —so don't get flustered if it's done at you, and do it wherever it could help to warn of your impending arrival. On such a ride, as the Amalfi coast road, you'll be glad you did ...

Driving in Rome. Only the most intrepid motorist stays cool in face of the Romans' hair-raising driving techniques. And, quite frankly, if it can be avoided, it's better for the jittery or inexperienced driver not to take the wheel in this city. Yet despite the surface impression of absolute chaos as you enter one of the city's busy squares there is a certain method in the apparent madness. Roman drivers are not reckless—

D simply attuned to a different concept of driving. If you observe the following ground rules and venture with prudence into the urban traffic whirlpool, you stand a good chance of coming out unscathed:

Glance around to your left and right and in your rear-view mirror all the time; the other drivers are doing the same, and they've developed quick reflexes.

Treat traffic lights which are theoretically in your favour and white lines across merging sidestreets with caution—don't take your priorities for granted.

To make progress in a traffic jam in one of Rome's squares, inch gently but confidently forward into the snarl-up. To wave on another driver, courteously letting him or her cut in ahead of you, is tantamount to abdicating your rights as a motorist.

However, traffic-free zones are tried out in various parts of town; these areas are constantly changing (but growing), and as at present, much of the city centre is under "trial". You'll see when you're there—another reason you're better off on foot!

Speed limits. Speed limits in Italy are based on the car engine size. The following chart gives the engine size in cubic centimetres and the speed limits (in kilometres per hour):

Engine size	less than 600 cc.	600 to 900 cc.	900 to 1,300 cc. (and motorcycles more than 150 cc.)	more than 1,300 cc.
Main roads	80 kph.	90 kph.	100 kph.	110 kph.
Motorways (Expressways)	90 kph.	110 kph.	130 kph.	140 kph.

Town speed limits are posted on the entry roads in kilometres per hour.

Parking. For motorized tourists as well as residents, parking is one of Rome's greatest challenges. Your very wisest course is to persevere on arrival until you find a parking spot near your hotel and then see the city on foot or by public transport, leaving your car unmoved until you depart from Rome.

There are formal, guarded parking areas operated by the Italian
110 Automobile Club (ACI), which are rather expensive; they're not

watched overnight. And Rome has a raft of freelance parking attendants who will offer to "guard" your car, even if illegally parked, for a fee. Double and triple-parking are astonishingly commonplace. Unfailingly take everything of value out of your car when leaving it on any Rome street at any hour, even in front of a police station (see CRIME). If you must drive within Rome, choose the siesta hours and the period between 10 p.m. and dawn, times when you'll easily find a legal parking space. The areas of central Rome recently closed, in theory, to traffic permit taxis, buses, residents' and commercial vehicles.

Fuel and oil. Fuel, sold at government-set price levels, comes as super (98–100 octane), lead-free (still rare, 95 octane) and normal (86–88 octane). Diesel is also usually available. Oil comes in at least three varieties.

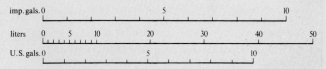

Traffic police *(polizia stradale).* When they're in evidence, which is rather infrequently, Italian traffic police use motorcycles or Alfa Romeos. All cities and many towns and villages have signs posted at the outskirts indicating the telephone number of the local traffic police headquarters or *carabinieri.* In recent years, spurred by the oil crisis and resulting austerity legislation, police have become somewhat stricter about speeding, an Italian national pastime. They also frown on the widespread practice of "jumping the light". Fines must often be paid on the spot. Ask for a receipt.

Breakdowns. Most service stations have a mechanic or someone who can make minor repairs, and garages are plentiful in Italy. Any can take care of a Fiat, and foreign makes have agencies in Rome. You can dial 116 for emergency service from the Automobile Club d'Italia. Call boxes are located at regular intervals on the *autostrada* in case of breakdowns or other emergencies.

Distance

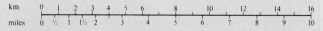

D **Road signs.** Most road signs employed in Italy are international pictographs, but here are some written ones you might come across:

Accendere le luci	Use headlights
Caduta massi	Falling rocks
Curva pericolosa	Dangerous bend (curve)
Deviazione	Diversion (Detour)
Discesa pericolosa	Steep hill (with gradient percentage)
Divieto di sorpasso	No overtaking (passing)
Divieto di sosta	No stopping
Lavori in corso	Road works (Men working)
Parcheggio autorizzato	Parking allowed
Passaggio a livello	Level railway crossing
Pericolo	Danger
Rallentare	Slow down
Senso vietato/unico	No entry/One-way street
Vietato l'ingresso	No entry
Zona pedonale	Pedestrian zone

(International) Driving Licence	**patente (internazionale)**
Car registration papers	**libretto di circolazione**
Green Card	**carta verde**
Can I park here?	**Posso parcheggiare qui?**
Are we on the right road for ...?	**Siamo sulla strada giusta per ...?**
Fill the tank please.	**Per favore, faccia il pieno.**
super/normal	**super/normale**
lead-free/diesel	**senza piombo/gasolio**
Check the oil/tires/battery.	**Controlli l'olio/i pneumatici/ la batteria.**
I've had a breakdown.	**Ho avuto un guasto.**
There's been an accident.	**C'è stato un incidente.**

DRUGS. Anyone possessing or selling drugs in Italy faces an unusually aroused police force and extremely severe legal penalties. No distinction is made between soft and hard drugs. Present maximum sentence is about eight years in prison and/or extremely stiff fines.

In every sense, drugs are a huge risk in Italy. Because of the monumental backlog in the nation's court cases, a person arrested on suspicion of a narcotics crime may spend as long as one year in jail before even being formally charged. Foreign consulates and embassies advise their citizens that there is no way for them to speed up the legal process.

ELECTRICITY *(elettricità)*. Electricity of two voltages—110–130 and 220—is supplied in Rome, with different plugs and sockets for each. The voltage is generally indicated on the sockets in hotels, but it's best to ask to avoid ruining your shaver or hairdryer.

What's the voltage, 220 or 110?	**Qual è il voltaggio, 220 (duecento-venti) o 110 (centodieci)?**
I'd like an adaptor/a battery.	**Vorrei una presa complementare/una batteria.**

EMERGENCIES. The Rome telephone service has many emergency numbers. The main ones are listed below. If you don't speak Italian, try to find a local resident to help you call.

Police, all-purpose emergency number	113
Ambulance and Red Cross	5100
Permanent day-time medical service	4 75 67 41
Medical service at home during the night	4 75 00 10
Fire	4 44 41
Road assistance (Automobile Club d'Italia)	116

Depending on the nature of the problem, see also separate entries such as CONSULATES AND EMBASSIES, MEDICAL CARE, POLICE, etc.

Careful	**Attenzione**	Police	**Polizia**
Fire	**Incendio**	Stop	**Stop**
Help	**Aiuto**	Stop thief	**Al ladro**

Please, can you place an emergency call for me to the …?	**Per favore, può fare per me una telefonata d'emergenza …?**
police	**alla polizia**
fire brigade	**ai pompieri**
hospital	**all'ospedale**

GUIDES and TOURS. Most hotels can arrange for multilingual guides or interpreters for any occasion. A selection is found in the yellow pages of the telephone directory under the entry "Traduzione", and Rome newspapers often carry advertisements offering such services. There are also guides near most of the major tourist attractions,

G and portable recorders with commentaries in English can often be hired. Another possibility is to contact the Sindacato Nazionale CISL Guide Turistiche, at Rampa Mignanelli, 12; tel. 6 78 98 42.

The Italian State Tourist Agency, CIT, and many private Italian and foreign firms offer excursions within Rome and to other points of interest, including Naples, Pompeii, Capri and the Amalfi Drive. Often, tourists are picked up and dropped off at their hotels. Your hotel receptionist will have a list of available guided group tours and will also know experienced private chauffeurs who take visitors on sightseeing tours by car.

We'd like an English-speaking guide.	**Desideriamo una guida che parla inglese.**
I need an English interpreter.	**Ho bisogno di un interprete d'inglese.**

H **HAIRDRESSERS and BARBERS** *(parrucchiere; barbiere)*. Rome overflows with these establishments for both men and women. But it's wise for ladies to telephone for an appointment (even then, you'll probably have to wait). Prices range from *haute coiffure* levels in the centre of Rome to very reasonable in the suburbs. Always ask beforehand or study the chart in the window before entering. As in most countries, the owner of a salon should never be tipped; the shampooer, manicurist or stylist should be tipped up to 15% of the bill. Most Rome hairdressing salons have facilities for facial treatment, make-up and massage.

I'd like a shampoo and set.	**Vorrei shampo e messa in piega.**
I want a ...	**Voglio ...**
haircut	**il taglio**
shave	**la rasatura**
blow-dry (brushing)	**asciugatura al fono**
permanent wave	**la permanente**
colour rinse	**un cachet**
manicure	**la manicure**
Don't cut it too short.	**Non li tagli troppo corti.**
A little more off (here).	**Un po' di più (qui).**

HITCH-HIKING *(autostop)*. Despite signs forbidding it at the entrances to the *autostrade*, hitch-hiking is common there and even within Rome (particularly when strikes bring public transport to a halt). Thousands of young people hitch-hike through Italy during the summer. A girl alone should not, though she's certain to get a ride instantly.

Can you give me a lift to …? **Può darmi un passaggio fino a …?**

LANGUAGE. Major Rome hotels and many shops in tourist areas employ personnel who speak passable English and French. Italian or imaginative sign language is essential in most of the city, though shopkeepers should know prices in English or French. Italians much appreciate a tourist's making an effort to speak their language, be it only a few words.

The Berlitz phrase book ITALIAN FOR TRAVELLERS covers most situations you are likely to encounter in Italy; also useful is the Italian-English/English-Italian pocket dictionary, containing a special menu-reader supplement.

Do you speak English? **Parla inglese?**
I don't speak Italian. **Non parlo italiano.**

LAUNDRY and DRY-CLEANING *(lavanderia; tintoria).* Rome has a growing number of laundromats where one either waits and watches the whirling machine or, for an extra charge, can leave washing with an attendant. Dry-cleaning and ironed washing are done by some laundromats. Otherwise, go to a *tintoria,* which will offer normal and express service. Most hotels will handle laundry and dry-cleaning, but rates are much higher.

When will it be ready? **Quando sarà pronto?**
I must have this for tomorrow **Mi serve per domani mattina.**
morning.

LOST PROPERTY. Cynics say that anything lost in Italy remains lost forever, but that's not necessarily true in Rome. Restaurants more often than not will have your forgotten briefcase, guide book or camera waiting for you at the cashier's desk. If you've lost something away from your hotel, have the receptionist call the lost property office *(Ufficio Oggetti Rinvenuti)*
tel. 8 816040, or go to the Via Bettoni, 1.

There are also lost property offices at the Termini railway station and at ATAC (the public transport organization) at Via Volturno, 65.

Lost documents should be reported to the police or your consulate.

Lost children. If you lose a child in Rome, forget your worst or even your mildly upsetting fears: report to the nearest police or *carabinieri* 115

L station where, almost certainly, a Roman will be towing in your young-ster before you finish your tale.

I've lost my passport/wallet/handbag.	**Ho perso il passaporto/portafoglio/la borsetta.**

M **MAPS** *(pianta; carta topografica)*. News-stands and tourist offices have a large selection of maps at a wide range of prices. Some are old (look for the date of publication in a corner of the map), and others may have pretty symbols of the Colosseum and St. Peter's but hope-lessly distort urban proportions. It's particularly important to have an up-to-date map if you're interested in city bus routes—they and the network of one-way streets change occasionally. The maps in this travel guide were prepared by Falk-Verlag, Hamburg, which also publishes a complete map of Rome.

a street plan of Rome	**una piantina di Roma**

MEDICAL CARE. If your health insurance does not honour bills from foreign countries, you can take out a special short-term policy for your trip. Visitors from Great Britain have the right to claim public health services available to Italians since both countries are members of the E.E.C. Before leaving home get a copy of the Form No. E111 from the Department of Health and Social Security.

If you're in need of medical care, it's best to ask your hotel recep-tionist to help you find a doctor (or dentist) who speaks English.

The first-aid *(pronto soccorso)* section of municipal hospitals can handle medical emergencies satisfactorily. Call 113 for an ambulance. Other emergency telephone numbers are listed in the entry EMER-GENCIES.

Pharmacies. The Italian *farmacia* is open during shopping hours, and in each district of Rome one operates at night and on weekends. The opening schedule for duty pharmacies is posted on every pharmacy door and in the local papers.

I need a doctor/a dentist.	**Ho bisogno di un medico/dentista.**
I've a pain here.	**Ho un dolore qui.**
a stomach ache	**il mal di stomaco**
a fever	**la febbre**
a sunburn/sunstroke	**una scottatura di sole/un colpo di sole**

MEETING PEOPLE. Although young women in Rome are more "liberated" than girls in most of Italy, almost all live with their families until marriage, which restricts social opportunities. There are a few discotheques and cafés, however, where single girls may be encountered. But conversation would most likely have to be in Italian.

Foreign women will have absolutely no trouble in finding an Italian companion: during the tourist season, the young men of Rome indulge in their favourite sport—seeking to pick up foreign girls who are presumed to be easier conquests. Some of their techniques include offering to guide a girl around town, taking her picture in front of a monument, showing her a special shop with bargains, or even falling on their knees to demonstrate the effects of her beauty. If you're not interested, ignore completely any approach, and don't start talking—even a sharp answer will be considered a sign of interest.

MONEY MATTERS

Currency. Italy's monetary unit is the *lira* (plural *lire,* abbreviated *L.* or *Lit.*).
Coins: L. 10, 20, 50, 100, 200 and 500.
Banknotes: L. 500, 1,000, 2,000, 5,000, 10,000, 50,000 and 100,000.
For currency restrictions, see CUSTOMS AND ENTRY REGULATIONS.

Banking hours are from 8.30 a.m. to 1.30 p.m., Monday to Friday.

Currency exchange offices *(cambio)* normally reopen later in the afternoon, and some operate on Saturdays. On Sundays, exchange windows at the airports and at Termini railway station are usually open. A *cambio* gives a slightly better rate for hard currency than a bank; but most of the time, you'll lose money by changing it at your hotel.

Traveller's cheques. All major traveller's cheques are accepted around Rome, though it's advisable to change them at a *cambio* (currency exchange) or at a bank, where you receive a higher rate of exchange than in stores or restaurants. Passports are usually required when changing currency and traveller's cheques.

Eurocheques are easily cashed in Italy.

M   **Credit cards.** Most hotels and bigger restaurants and shops accept credit cards. When hiring a car the deposit is waived if you have a recognized card.

Prices. Cinemas and horse-drawn carriages are expensive, concerts and taxi fares reasonable, discotheques and nightclubs often ruinous, museums and art galleries surprisingly cheap (and free on Sundays). In bars or cafés, sitting down and having a waiter bring your espresso may cost three times as much as having it at the counter. Certain prices are listed on page 98 to give you a relative idea of what things cost.

I want to change some pounds/dollars.	**Desidero cambiare delle sterline/dei dollari.**
Do you accept traveller's cheques?	**Accetta traveller's cheques?**
Can I pay with this credit card?	**Posso pagare con la carta di credito?**
How much is this?	**Quanto costa questo?**

MOTORSCOOTER HIRE. There's only one place in Rome where you can hire motorscooters and mopeds:

Scoot-a-long, Via Cavour, 302; tel. 6 78 02 06

It's impossible to hire bicycles in the capital, but you'll most likely have more luck on the coast.

N   **NEWSPAPERS and MAGAZINES** (*giornale; rivista*). Many major British and Continental newspapers and magazines are on sale at kiosks in the centre of Rome, at some hotels, at the Vatican and at the airport and railway station. London papers usually arrive in Rome on the afternoon of the day of publication. English-language periodicals are expensive. One of Rome's English-language newspapers, the *International Daily News*, which carries full U.S. stock-market quotations, is on sale everywhere early in the morning, from Tuesday to Sunday. Many news-stands stay open until 9 p.m., and one in Largo Argentina and two on Via Veneto past midnight. *This Week in Rome*, in English or Italian, is sold in tourist areas; it lists the week's events, some hotels and restaurants, entertainment, shops and church services.

Have you any English-language newspapers?	**Avete giornali in inglese?**

PHOTOGRAPHY. Rome, of course, is truly a photographer's delight, and even the rankest amateur will want to sightsee with a camera. In summer, Rome's late afternoon sun (after 3 p.m.) is best for quality of light and colour. Special permission is required to photograph art works in a minority of the city's museums and churches. Ask at the entrance.

All major brands and sizes of film are obtainable in Rome, but prices are higher than in most other countries. Development and printing is up to international standards.

I'd like a film for this camera.	**Vorrei una pellicola per questa macchina fotografica.**
a black and white film	**una pellicola in bianco e nero**
a colour-slide film	**una pellicola per diapositive**
a film for colour prints	**una pellicola per fotografie a colori**
35-mm film	**una pellicola trentacinque millimetri**
super-8	**super otto**
How long will it take to develop this film?	**Quanto tempo ci vuole per sviluppare questa pellicola?**
May I take a picture?	**Posso fare una fotografia?**

POLICE (polizia, carabinieri). Rome's municipal police, dressed in navy blue with white helmets or all-white with shiny buttons, handle traffic and other routine police tasks. While rarely speaking any foreign language, they're courteous and as helpful as possible to tourists. For polizia headquarters, telephone 46 86 or, in an emergency, 113.

The carabinieri (paramilitary police), who may wear brown or blue uniforms, deal with serious crimes and demonstrations. The carabinieri telephone number is 212121. Rome has 6,500 policemen but you'd never know it during siesta.

Where's the nearest police station?	**Dov'è il più vicino posto di polizia?**

PUBLIC HOLIDAYS (festa). On all holidays, banks, government institutions, most shops and at least some museums are closed. During Ferragosto in August almost everything in Rome shuts down except hotels, a very few shops, farmacie, cafés and restaurants, and some of the major sightseeing attractions.

P

January 1	*Capodanno* or *Primo dell'Anno*	New Year's Day
April 25	*Festa della Liberazione*	Liberation Day
May 1	*Festa del Lavoro*	Labour Day
August 15	*Ferragosto*	Assumption Day
November 1	*Ognissanti*	All Saints' Day
December 8	*L'Immacolata Concezione*	Immaculate Conception
December 25	*Natale*	Christmas Day
December 26	*Santo Stefano*	St. Stephen's Day
Movable date:	*Lunedì di Pasqua*	Easter Monday

R **RADIO and TV** *(radio; televisione).* During the tourist season, RAI, the Italian state radio and TV network, occasionally broadcasts news in English, predominantly about Italian affairs. Vatican Radio carries foreign-language religious news programmes at various times during the day. Shortwave radio reception is excellent throughout the night and part of the day. RAI television broadcasts only in Italian.

RELIGIOUS SERVICES. A few Catholic churches celebrate mass in English, and major non-Catholic denominations have churches in Rome, often with services in English. Details are published in *Rome Daily American, International Daily News* and *This Week in Rome* on sale in most hotels and at news-stands throughout the city. The main synagogue is located on Lungotevere dei Cenci.

Mass is celebrated at St. Peter's Basilica at no set times on week-days, except on Thursdays, when there's a pilgrims' mass at 9.30 a.m. On Sundays high mass is at 10 a.m., on the last two Sundays of the month at 1 p.m. and 5 p.m., in winter at 4 p.m. Services in languages other than Italian are held at times in side chapels within the basilica. You'll have to check on the spot for hours.

S **SIESTA.** The pressures of modern times are catching up with Rome: no longer is the siesta a sacred tradition. The modern business day is gradually creeping in, with a nonstop day affecting many (even most) commerces in central Rome. Nevertheless there's a kind of drowsy feel about the hours just after lunch, when public transport runs fitfully and everything operates in low gear. You'd probably do well to keep to the civilized habit of a siesta nap—especially since most shops stay open till about 8 p.m. Restaurants permit diners to linger at table until 3 o'clock or even later.

TIME DIFFERENCES. Italy follows Central European Time (GMT +1), and from April to September clocks are put one hour ahead (= GMT+ 2). Summer time chart:

New York	London	Italy	Jo'burg	Sydney	Auckland
6 a.m.	11 a.m.	**noon**	noon	8 p.m.	10 p.m.

What time is it?   **Che ore sono?**

TIPPING. Though a service charge is added to most restaurant bills, it is customary to leave an additional tip. It is also in order to hand the bellboys, doormen, hat check attendants, garage attendants, etc., a coin or two for their service.

The chart below gives some suggestions as to what to leave.

Hotel porter, per bag	L. 1,000
Maid, per day	L. 1,000
Lavatory attendant	L. 300
Waiter	10%
Taxi driver	10%
Hairdresser/Barber	up to 15%
Tourist guide	10%

TOILETS. You'll find public toilets in most museums and galleries; restaurants, bars, cafés and large stores usually have facilities; airports and train stations always do. You'll also find toilets at service stations along the motorways. They may be designated in different ways: W.C. (for water closet) with the picture of a man or woman; sometimes the wording will be in Italian—*Uomini* (men) or *Donne* (women). The most confusing label for foreigners is *Signori* (men—with a final *i*) and *Signore* (women—with a final *e*).

Where are the toilets?   **Dove sono i gabinetti?**

T **TOURIST INFORMATION OFFICES.** The Italian State Tourist Offices *(Ente Nazionale Italiano per il Turismo,* abbreviated E.N.I.T.) are found in Italy and abroad. They publish detailed brochures with up-to-date information on accommodation, means of transport and other general tips and useful addresses all over Italy.

Italian State Tourist Offices

Canada. 3, place Ville-Marie, Suite 22, Montreal 13, P.Q., tel. (514) 849-83 51

Eire. 47, Merrion Square, Dublin 2, tel. (01) 766-397

United Kingdom. 1, Princes Street, London WIR 7RA; tel. (01) 408–1254

U.S.A. 500 N. Michigan Avenue, Chicago, IL 60611, tel. (312) 644-09 90
630 Fifth Avenue, New York, NY 10020, tel. (212) 245-4961/4
St. Francis Hotel, 360 Post Street, San Francisco, CA 94108, tel. (415) 392-5266

In **Rome,** the E.N.I.T. office is in Via Marghera, 2; tel. 4 97 11.

The Provincial Tourist Boards *(Ente Provinciale per il Turismo,* abbreviated E.P.T.), located in each major town in Italy, offer information on accommodation, camping and regional events.

E.P.T. offices in Rome:

Via Parigi, 11; tel. 46 18 51
Via Parigi, 5; tel. 46 37 48 (Tourists' Assistance Centre)
Termini railway station, tel. 46 54 61
Fiumicino (Leonardo da Vinci) airport, tel. 6 01 12 55

TRANSPORT

Underground (subway)*. Rome has two underground railway lines *(metropolitana,* or *metrò).* One runs from the main railway station, Termini, with stops at the Colosseum, EUR, Ostia Antica and Ostia Lido. The bisecting *metrò* line, inaugurated in 1980, runs from Via Ottaviano near the Vatican and south-east to Via Anagnina. This line, about 25 kilometres long, has 22 stations and passes under most of Rome's popular tourist sights. Tickets are sold at most news-stands and tobacconists, or can be purchased from machines at the stations.

Buses* *(autobus).* Service is frequent during the day with skeleton night services. News-stands sell maps showing the major bus routes, which often change. Routes are well indicated on green-and-white signs at every bus stop *(fermata)*, and on the vehicles themselves the number, starting point and destination are shown. Within Rome the fare is standard, irrespective of the distance travelled. Tickets for most buses must be purchased at bars, tobacconists or news-stands.

Most buses from Rome to other Italian cities depart from points near the Termini railway station.

Weekly and monthly tickets, good for part of or for the entire public transport network 24 hours a day, are available at the ATAC (Rome's public transport organization) office at Largo Giovanni Montemartini near Termini railway station. There are also special tourist tickets valid for specific periods of unlimited travel.

Taxis* *(tassì* or *taxi).* Rome's taxis, which remain rather cheap by European and American standards, may be hailed in the street, picked up at any of the dozens of taxi ranks or obtained by telephone. The yellow pages of the telephone directory, under "Taxi", lists all of Rome's ranks. Cabs are yellow and operate with a meter which a passenger should always make sure is running. Extra charges for luggage and for night, holiday or airport trips are posted in four languages inside all taxis. The airport surcharge is high—several thousand lire. A tip of at least 10% is customary. Non-metered *taxi pirati* charge two to three times the normal taxi rates for trips in their private cars.

Radio taxi, phone 35 70/47 74/38 75/84 43.

Horse-cabs *(carrozza).* A familiar sight in Rome for centuries, horse-drawn carriages now, sadly, number only a few dozen. Often to be found at such tourist haunts as St. Peter's Square, the Spanish Steps, the Trevi Fountain and the Via Veneto, the horse-cabs theoretically have meters (usually "accidentally" concealed beneath a horse blanket), but in fact one should agree on a price with the driver before trotting off. They're vastly more expensive than other forms of urban transport, but—except during rush hours—also vastly more pleasant. Children, of course, adore a *carrozza* ride.

Trains *(treno).* The following list describes the various types of trains:

TEE	The international Trans Europ Express, first class only with surcharge; seat reservations essential.

T

Intercity (IC)	Inter-city express with very few stops; a luxury international service with first ans second class.
Rapido (R)	Long-distance express train stopping at major cities only; first and second class.
Espresso (EXP)/ Direttissimo	Long-distance train, stopping at main stations.
Diretto (D)	Slower than the *Espresso,* it makes a number of local stops.
Locale (L)	Local train which stops at almost every station.
Accelerato (A)	Same as a *Locale.*
Littorina	Small diesel train used on short runs.

Carozza ristorante Dining car	*Vagone letto* Sleeping car with individual compartments and washing facilities	*Carozza cuccette* Sleeping berth car (couchette); blankets and pillows	*Bagagliaio* Guard's van (baggage car); normally only registered luggage permitted

Tickets can be purchased and reservations made at a local travel agency or at the railway station. Better-class trains almost always have dining-cars which offer wine, beer, mineral water and decent if unimaginative food at reasonable prices. All trains have toilets and washing facilities of varying quality. Lacking a reservation, it's wise to arrive at the station at least 20 minutes before departure to ensure a seat: Italy's trains are often very crowded.

Where is the nearest bus stop/ underground station?	**Dov'è la fermata d'autobus/la stazione della metropolitana più vicina?**
When's the next bus/train to …?	**Quando parte il prossimo autobus/treno per …?**
I want a ticket to …	**Vorrei un biglietto per …**
single (one-way)	**andata**
return (round-trip)	**andata e ritorno**

WATER *(acqua).* Rome's drinking water, not least from its outdoor fountains, is famous for its flavour and perfectly safe. Nonetheless, the usual custom is to have bottled mineral water as well as wine with a meal, rather than tap water. Mineral waters, a national obsession, are popularly believed to help not only digestion, but an incredible array of afflictions—about whose alleged properties medical opinion is sharply divided. If tap water should not be drunk, there will be a sign reading, *acqua non potabile.*

I'd like a bottle of mineral water.	**Vorrei una bottiglia di acqua minerale.**
fizzy (carbonated)/still	**gasata/naturale**

SOME USEFUL EXPRESSIONS

yes/no	**sì/no**
please/thank you	**per favore/grazie**
excuse me/you're welcome	**mi scusi/prego**
where/when/how	**dove/quando/come**
how long/how far	**quanto tempo/quanto dista**
yesterday/today/tomorrow	**ieri/oggi/domani**
day/week/month/year	**giorno/settimana/mese/anno**
left/right	**sinistra/destra**
up/down	**su/giù**
good/bad	**buono/cattivo**
big/small	**grande/piccolo**
cheap/expensive	**buon mercato/caro**
hot/cold	**caldo/freddo**
open/closed	**aperto/chiuso**
free (vacant)/occupied	**libero/occupato**
near/far	**vicino/lontano**
early/late	**presto/tardi**
right/wrong	**giusto/sbagliato**
I don't understand.	**Non capisco.**
Waiter/Waitress, please.	**Cameriere!/Cameriera!** (or **Senta!** = "listen")
I'd like …	**Vorrei …**
How much is that?	**Quant'è?**

Index

An asterisk (*) next to a page number indicates a map reference. For index to Practical Information, see page 99.